SPIRIT OF AN OUTLAW

The Untold Story of Tupac Amaru Shakur and Yaki 'Kadafi' Fula

Photos and History by
Yaasmyn Fula

Foreword by Quincy Jones

Bearded Dragon Books
Los Angeles

Túpac Amaru II (revolutionary fighter from Peru and who Tupac was named after) and Tupac Amaru Shakur, two views. Drawing by Bradford Brown, ca 2000.

For all the kindred spirits in the world who toil in the darkness to save Mother Earth and all her creatures.

© 2020 by Yaasmyn Fula; all rights reserved.

No part of this book may be reproduced in any manner (written, electronic, recording, photocopying, etc.) without written permission of the publisher or author. The exception would be in the case of brief quotations embodied in the critical articles or reviews and pages where permission is specifically granted by the publisher or author.

Although every precaution has been taken to verify the accuracy of the information contained herein, the author and publisher assume no responsibility for any errors or omissions. No liability is assumed for damages that may result from the use of information contained within.

Bearded Dragon Books, Los Angeles

For wholesale and other inquiries, visit SpiritofanOutlaw.com

Front Cover Photo: Yaasmyn Fula

Back Cover Photo: Chi Modu

Cover Design: AmeriCalifornia StudioWorks

Interior Layout: Lily J. Noonan

ISBN: 978-1733140003 (print), 978-1733140010 (digital)

Library of Congress Control Number: 2019919206

10 9 8 7 6 5 4 3 2

Printed in the United States of America

Contents

- Foreword by Quincy Jones
- Introduction from the author
- 1   Sons Rize - Rites of Passage
- 19   Circle of Women
- 27   Billy Garland - Redemption
- 29   Bronx Legal Services - Serving the People
- 38   Lincoln Hospital - Ground Zero
- 41   West Side - The Call
- 51   Metropolitan Correctional Center
- 65   Sekou Odinga - Yaki's Father
- 71   The 80s - Pied Piper
- 85   Digital Underground
- 87   Evolution of The Outlawz
- 93   The Big Picture
- 103   Picture Me Rollin'
- 107   Atlanta - Lock, Stock, and Barrel
- 111   Trial - The Setup
- 118   Clinton Prison - The Ordeal
- 127   Death Row - Dark Forces
- 133   Euphanasia - The Road Back
- 139   Vegas - The Vigil
- 141   Son Rize, Volume 1
- 154   Legacy & Lessons

Author Yaasmyn Fula and Quincy Jones, Los Angeles.

FOREWARD

*B*ack in 1995, in an effort to create bridges of peace amongst the hip-hop community, I hosted "The Quincy Jones Hip-Hop Symposium" in New York. My hope for the event and plea to the entire generation was to simply stop the violence. The lives of these kids were incredibly precious and they were too young and too smart to be caught up in the crossfire. I had Dr. Dre, Common, P. Diddy, Alan Kaye, Clarence Avant, Ed Lewis, and many more in attendance, and I also asked Colin Powell to speak, because I wanted the kids to hear from the people who had "been there done that." Standing there in the conference room with all of those young faces staring up at me, with bright eyes full of unrealized potential, I couldn't help but get emotional when I spoke about the recent murder of Tupac (who would have been my soon-to-be son-in-law). All of the losses hurt, but that one hit close to home; the bullets were real, and I wanted the hip-hop community to wake up, because they couldn't afford to be non-political.

After the horrendous deaths of Tupac in September 1996 and Yaasmyn Fula's son, Yaki, in November 1996, we were all devastated. Back-to-back sorrow. During this time, my daughter, Kidada, suggested that I ask Yaasmyn to come work for me to help provide a space for Yaasmyn to get back on her feet. And man, I'm telling you, it was as if the heavens brought us together.

My life was more hectic than usual at the time—I was in the middle of running my film and television production company; a record label; a magazine enterprise, Vibe; Q Radio; the Listen Up Foundation; home-building initiatives with Habitat for Humanity and South Africa; and more. Because of my high-paced life, I needed someone who had the fortitude to wear many hats. More importantly, I needed someone who understood the history of my company, had the ultimate organizational skills, and was willing to help get everything on track. That person was none other than Yaasmyn. This young lady had not only been with Tupac from birth, but was a positive influence his entire life, survived the Black Panther Party, managed his office, buried both sons—and was still standing! Those, in and of themselves, were incredible life credentials and she did not disappoint as she assumed her role in the office. In the midst of our sorrow and pain, we shared an emotional resurrection as we slowly but surely rebuilt the structure of not only my businesses, but our lives.

Without understanding the genesis of Tupac Amaru Shakur, his entire life is up for misinterpretation. His vision to end suffering and poverty was not a spur of the moment decision; it was embedded into his art and he was keenly aware of how music played a role in shaping culture. We had many discussions on this subject as I too shared with him my life story of growing up on the South Side of Chicago. I reminded him of the history of bebop, R&B, and the emergence of jazz and hip-hop as musical and artistic expressions of a dark period of racial hostility. Hip-hop was nothing new, but he brought something new to it.

Despite our generational differences, we shared a common purpose to reach people through the power of music. As a young kid, I had the great fortune of being mentored by a great deal of special individuals who took me under their wings, such as Clark Terry, Count Basie, Benny Carter, and Lionel Hampton. I wanted to pass the same wisdom that nurtured me as a young trumpeter on the road with great musicians, down to the likes of Tupac, in whom I had recognized a great deal of talent and potential. We talked about working together, and he first sampled a song from *Body Heat* to use on his album, *All Eyez On Me*. We had plans. His future was so bright. And beyond that, he had a great support system which Yaasmyn was undoubtedly the foundation of.

Having known Yaasmyn for so many years, I always knew she had a powerful story to tell, so it absolutely makes my soul smile to know that her heart, soul, and stories about the life of her and her precious sons have found their way onto these pages. All artists are outlaws in some way, shape, or form; we're always breaking the rules, and if we're not, we're probably playing it too safe. You've got to master the rules before you can break them! Tupac and Yaki left their mark on the world and I know that Yaasmyn will do their spirits justice as she shares their untold stories in *Spirit of an Outlaw*.

Quincy Jones

INTRODUCTION

𝒯his is the story of the childhood bond between Tupac Amaru Shakur and Yafeu "Yaki Kadafi" Fula. Both sons of the social revolution in America in the 70s and 80s, they captured the hearts and souls of a generation and continue to have a global presence.

What has been written by others belies the truth of their special bond, trivializing it as mere "friends." This book unveils their lifelong brotherhood and the adoration shared by each since childhood. It is also a testimonial to the power of love and the profound effect Tupac and Yaki had upon the lives of so many. Their story has all the attributes of a modern-day Shakespearean tragedy—loyalty, kinship, courage, and betrayal.

These photos and stories connect the dots of the period they grew up in with the people and events that molded their consciousness. You may have seen some of these photos before on the internet by people I have shared them with. With this book, you will now know about the moments that led up to and surrounded each of these photos. Over the years, many images were confiscated by the FBI during my ongoing battle against their tactics and efforts to silence and neutralize the voices of those who fought for justice.

This is not just a photo book. This is a documentary of social justice, injustice, and cultural movements that shows the influence on the lives of two young boys who later impacted an entire generation.

Each photo captures a moment to tell a piece of their story. It was a challenge from the day they were born to get them to pose or in many instances to even have a moment to focus my 35mm camera, which was always by my side. I apologize if some photos are blurred. Though blurred, these photos capture the fullness of their spirit.

Tupac and Yaki at YMCA Camp, Montclair, NJ, ca 1985. If you look closely you can see Tupac had braces on his teeth. He always had problems with his teeth as a result of his mom's incarceration during pregnancy.

Tupac was six years older than Yaki and became his surrogate father, brother, and mentor because Yaki's father, Sekou, fled underground during the Panther 21 trials in 1969. Tupac taught Yaki many things about the struggle, about courage, and the importance of being strong and proud. They were inseparable in life and in death… our very own Butch Cassidy and the Sundance Kid.

Yaki learned his lessons well. He lived without fear his entire life—SANS PEUR. Even in his last breath, Yaki's final exclamation to his killer was an act of defiance when a bullet extinguished his life on November 10, 1996, just two months after the murder of his beloved brother. To live eternally in the hearts and minds of the people is to have lived a good life.

However, the special bond of brotherhood shared between Yaki and Tupac remains obscured today more than twenty years after their deaths. It is little wonder their bond has been overlooked, given the falsities that abound about Tupac and his story. The revolutionary legacy inherited by Tupac and brilliantly passed on to his little brother Yaki was the foundation of their relationship and is captured in this memoir.

FROM THE DAY YAKI WAS BORN, TUPAC LAID HIS ARMS AROUND HIM, NURTURED HIM, AND PROTECTED HIM.

Tupac Amaru Shakur was named after a revolutionary resistance movement in Peru. The Túpac Amaru revolutionaries resisted Christianity and the Spanish occupation in the 1500s. When one was killed, the namesakes picked up the cry for liberation in the next generation. When the son was murdered by Spanish colonizers, the great-grandson continued the revolts against the conquistadors. The Spanish thought they killed the last of the royal Inca family when they killed Túpac Amaru I in 1572. But in 1780, his great-grandson, Túpac Amaru II, picked up the banner of revolt against the colonizers.

The birth of Tupac Amaru Shakur on June 16, 1971, was an extension to that chain of resistance against conquest and domination—a descendant of the people's righteous quest for justice and peace; only this time, it was to be on the shores of North America.

By naming Tupac after a revolutionary movement, Afeni wanted Tupac to always have a broad horizon to chart his course. The resistance movement for freedom and peace was global and it was very important Tupac understood he was connected by movements, not by neighborhoods.

Tupac and Yaki were characters in a larger story. Tupac connected the anger and rage of an entire generation to a political consciousness whose global presence remains today, more than twenty years later. They cannot be replaced for they sprung from the revolutionary fervor and DNA of ancestral laws. Their deaths created a profound shift in the heart and soul of hip hop.

(opposite) Tupac with his arms around Yaki, Bronx, NY outside his Aunt Gloria's home, ca '79.

Tupac, Yaki, and me attending a birthday party.

This book is also a tribute to Tupac's namesake—the Peruvian resistance movement—and to all the resistance movements that nurtured the revolutionary spirit of Tupac Amaru Shakur and the indomitable spirit of love for all people he shared with my son, Yaki. The true legacy of Tupac must continue and should not be overshadowed with self-serving epitaphs and fictionalized versions of his life and death. He was a warrior child who accepted the baton passed to him. He was not infallible. He had the audacity to be fearless as he evolved; he was introspective but short on time as he boldly chartered a course to resurrect the soul of his generation, while placing his own in harm's way. It was perfectly fitting for him to be named after the Túpac Amaru Inca revolutionary dynasty in Peru that fought the 18th century Spanish invaders.

Tupac was Yaki's protector, his guardian. After Tupac's murder, Yaki no longer had his beloved brother to protect him when the predators were lying in the darkness ready to pounce on him, vulnerable and unprotected. In the end, Tupac and Yaki were both betrayed by people who to this day are incapable of understanding the depth of their treachery.

Yaki and Tupac were sons of revolutionaries. They sprung from the loins of Black Panther mothers and fathers dedicated to the teachings of Malcolm X, Sojourner Truth, and James Baldwin. They were taught at a very early age about the revolutionary legacy they inherited—the sacrifices and the responsibilities. They are the descendants of a legacy of resistance and struggle for dignity for all people. Their legacy is rooted in the struggle for human rights, independence, and freedom for all people to live in peace. Their story must be told from the bowels and blood of the people that cradled their revolutionary consciousness and breathed life into their souls, not from those who dare claim them as property, carving up their carcasses, distorting the legacy and shoulders that catapulted them to greatness. Their ties are to African ancestors and all indigenous people who suffer from the whip of colonization, treaty violations, and those who resist unjustified grabs of their land, water, and natural resources. They were our sons who we raised to understand they exist due to great sacrifices from the ancestors and they must always promote the interest of the people first and foremost.

Within these pages, I repudiate the false narratives from the media of Tupac and Yaki and shed light on the truth of the revolutionary cord that bound their hearts. Tupac was keenly aware of his revolutionary inheritance and his namesake Peruvian brothers in arms. Any portrayal of Tupac that does not illuminate his revolutionary consciousness, his revolutionary upbringing, and the people who put him in touch with his soul's purpose is a betrayal to his legacy.

The manipulation of the cultural legacy of black musicians and artists is nothing new. Tupac brought his art and poetry into existence using music as the medium to organize the people to resist domination

(opposite) Celebration of Tupac's movie Juice; Washington Heights, NY, '93.

(this page) Tupac holding his cassette tape 2Pacalypse Now with Yaki wearing 2Pacalypse hat, ca '93.

and control. His art and his message resonated in the hearts of youth globally because he railed against the exploitation of people of color all over the world. It is a travesty to portray Tupac in any light other than who he really was—a soldier marching in the footprints of Malcolm X, James Baldwin, Nat Turner, and Denmark Vessey.

Through my photos and words, you will learn the story of the special bond shared by two young boys born under the star of revolution and constricted by fate. Throughout their lives, I wore many hats. I was auntie, mother, father, nursemaid, chauffeur, advisor, godmother, bodyguard, and consigliere. Tupac was Yaki's brother at times, his father at other times, but through it all, Tupac was always his protector. Some say Tupac and Yaki were star-crossed, ill fated. In life, as in death, they were inseparable. Their bond was one of blood brothers, but stronger than just blood.

Tupac courageously accepted the baton of resistance and used the microphone to raise the consciousness of an entire generation. It is clear today that there is still much to share with the world and to the fans, how special they were.

For those who listened to the music of Tupac and Yaki and experienced profound change in their lives, this book is for you.

For all the thousands of people who reached out to me from all over the world sending respect and expressing adoration for my sons, this memoir is for you.

I seek to give dignity to each breath of life they shared, which was filled with pure love. Despite the shroud of conspiracy and lies that surrounded their deaths, their impact on our lives is everlasting. Truth has a way of resurrecting from the ashes of deceit. History has already made provisions for this inevitability.

May their flames forever continue to inspire and motivate future generations.

On the steps of an apartment building in the Bronx, around the time UNLV sports shirts were popular. Yaki always wanted whatever Tupac was wearing Yaki was growing up fast; here he was a few inches taller than Tupac and he loved it.

Sons Rize - Rites of Passage

In the tumultuous post-civil rights era of the Birmingham Church bombings, assassination of Malcolm X, and dismantling of the Black Panther Party, the survivors arose from the ashes to sing lullabies of faith and resistance. Tupac's strong cultural identity sprung from the ballads he learned from heroes and heroines whose examples of courage gave him sustenance. Even in these dark hours, we never stopped organizing people to become unified and connected. In the transitory nature of the different ideologies from civil rights to human rights to anti-war protests to black liberation, Tupac was present throughout each evolutionary stage. He bore witness to ordinary people accomplishing extraordinary feats of survival. He witnessed firsthand how people and movements are all connected. The anti-imperialist, anti-war movement was connected to and worked with the anti-slavery, anti-drug movements. Tupac saw how people from all walks of life came together to protest the conditions of poverty and racial degradation to build thriving communities. Through it all, he enlightened and uplifted everyone in his presence.

Tupac was not my son, but still I mothered him. I knew him long before the day he was born.

Along with many others, I marched in front of the Women's House of Detention

(above) Son Rize Vol. 1, produced in 2005 by Donny Rizz of Cold Flow Productions. It is a tribute to Yaki and Tupac's lives and memorializes those who came before them. The album cover shows the 1968 photo (also shown to the right) of Yaki's father, Sekou Odinga, marching with the Black Panther Party.

(opposite) Black Panthers marching to a news conference in NYC to protest the Huey P. Newton trial, July 22, 1968. Yaki's father is the one in the middle with sunglasses holding the Free Huey banner, looking upward. Credit MPI/Stringer, Getty Images.

where Afeni was incarcerated during the Panther 21 trial, demanding that her captors allow her prenatal care, milk, and a suitable diet, all of which was being denied by the New York State Department of Corrections. We marched outside the courtroom at 100 Centre Street, NYC, where his mother Afeni, pregnant with him, fought for his life and hers during the Panther 21 trial.

The jury panel for the Panther 21 trial was comprised of twelve intelligent and thoughtful people. The jury foreman was a composer named Ingram Fox; Juror #4, Ed Kennebeck, was an editor at Viking Press; and there was a carpenter, to mention a few. They delivered not guilty verdicts after deliberating only three hours. Honestly, it took longer to deliver the 156 not guilty verdicts for the thirteen defendants.

After Afeni was finally acquitted, she moved into a flat with other socially conscious women. One of those women was Karen Kadison, who was a regular traveler to Peru. It was Karen who shared the stories and history of the Túpac Amaru revolutionaries with Afeni.

Tupac was born on June 16, 1971, a month and a couple of days after Afeni's acquittal in the New York Panther 21 trial. We were so happy he was not going to be born in jail!

He was a hellraiser from birth, like the lyrics from the song "Cradle to the Grave" on the *Thug Life* album.

June 16, 1971, Mama gave birth to a hell raisin' heavenly son
See the doctor tried to smack me
But I smacked him back
My first words were "Thug for life" and "Papa, pass the Mac."

Tupac possessed an emotional intensity that was undeniably powerful. As a fetus, he felt the vibrations of his mother as she defended herself, cross-examined informants, and sang songs to District Attorney Phillips during the Panther 21 trial. He felt the frequent instances of injustice rage through the placenta that nurtured him during the longest trial in the history of New York.

We knew when he was born that HE KNEW we fought for his life. His energy was kinetic, atomic, solar—like he was plugged in.

All of the things that happened as Afeni carried him in her womb must have had this electric effect on him. It was as if he were taking notes. There was no other explanation for his kinetic energy at birth, a magnetism that remained with him throughout his life. In his infancy, we all took turns cradling Pac, trying to assuage his temperament. He was enraged and wild, yet, more often, he was also consumed with enormous and bountiful joy. How easily he wore out whichever devoted handler attempted to contain his gleeful protestations. We passed him around and prayed as we surrendered him to each set of loving arms. But it was only Afeni who could take him in her arms with his little body flailing wildly, look him in his eyes, and in a soft voice sing his favorite song, Roberta Flack's "No Way to Say Goodbye" which had the effect of calming his wild energy. Afeni taught him, "You are our black prince. You are my miracle and you will make black people proud…"

During Tupac's earliest years, things were still very hectic in the streets. The Panther Party was fractionalized; the divisions created by the FBI antagonized the feuding between East Coast/West Coast groups and had deadly results. Many lost their lives due to petty animosities and falling victim to the same predatory behavior we fought so hard to stop. Afeni often sought refuge across the water with us in New Jersey just to get away from the New York mayhem. Sometimes we would go over to her pad in the village and provide security for her and the newborn Tupac due to the war going on between Panther factions. Soon, they moved in with us in our apartment on North Arlington Avenue in East Orange, NJ. It was safer.

The music of the 70s consoled us and became our marching songs as we organized the people, raised our sons, and survived America. Tupac's favorite song, one that we played over and over, was "Black Seeds Keep on Growing" by The Main Ingredient.

The song became an anthem for the movement. We played that song on the record player so much that the vinyl album wore out. We used to show Tupac the picture on the cover and tell him "Look Pac! You see that little boy climbing to the top? That's you!" He had survived the odds. We knew he was special and made sure he knew it, too. He used to grin his infamous smile from ear to ear and walk around the room in Pampers with the album jacket.

The children were always improvising music. Music was a great influence in all of our lives and they were exposed to the best artists of the time—Curtis Mayfield, The Main Ingredient, War, Sergio Mendes & Brasil 66, Tito Puente, Donny Hathaway, Mandrill, Laura Nyro, and Sarah Vaughan. The jazz greats—John Coltrane, Miles Davis, Charlie Parker, Etta James, Thelonious Monk, Rahsaan Roland Kirk, Charles Lloyd—played on our hi-fi turntables, too. Songs of protest sung by comrades like Chris Kando Iijima, Nobuko JoAnne Miyamoto, and William "Charlie" Chin who together created the album *A Grain of Sand: Music for the Struggle by Asians in America*, and Elaine Brown's "The End of Silence" accentuated Tupac's early listening repertoire. His musical exposure was as vast and as rich as the climate he was growing up in. He always loved music and no matter what he was doing would stop as soon as he heard a melody, an instrument and flash that enormous smile in sync with every beat.

FOOLED EVERYBODY AND YOU GREW UP BIG AND STRONG!

Black Seeds by The Main Ingredient (RCA 1971). It was the anthem we played to baby Tupac..."Fooled everybody and you grew up big and strong..." RIP Donald McPherson, lead singer and creative genius.

Photos from when we lived on Arlington Ave, East Orange, NJ

(opposite top) Tupac with bottle dangling from his mouth with his cousin Billy Lesane on the mic, as Scott Lesane looks on. The pail was turned over to improvise a drum which Tupac gleefully pounded to the beat of the music.

(opposite bottom) Tupac wearing Pampers and chasing a fleeing Sharonda Davila into the arms of her brother Tony. That boy chased Sharonda all over the house with arms open. All he ever wanted was a hug.

(top left) Tupac in pursuit again, this time with his trademark bottle he dangled from his mouth. Sharonda had chicken pox and Tupac was next in line, but it didn't stop him from chasing her, with her brother Tony to the rescue. Sep '72.

(top right) Baby Tupac picture, ca '74.

My dad migrated to this country with his family in 1910 from Jamaica. He is the side of the family that came to the shores of America having paid cash for their passage on a ship to Ellis Island. He was a tender, hard-working Jamaican maaan. My maternal grandmother, Delia Martin née Harrison, has ancestors that were traced to Cameroon. My maternal grandfather was Thomas Martin and his father, Charles Martin, was Lenape Indian-Delaware Nation, which made him an indigenous American.

The camera sometimes gave double exposures. The photo below shows my father holding baby Yaki and to the right in this photo is the handcrafted wood bassinet that Pac slept in as a baby. This wasn't any bassinet though. It was carved from pure love.

During the Panther 21 trial, unbeknown to us, the carpenter who was part of the jury was whittling away during the eight-month trial, creating a wooden cradle for baby Tupac. He presented it to Afeni at the end of the trial. It was a work of art. We rocked that boy in that cradle many nights as it had been carefully constructed so that the base could swing. After Tupac grew out of it, Afeni kept that cradle and passed it on to me when Yaki was born.

Yafeu Akiyele Fula was born October 9, 1977, at St. Luke's Hospital on Amsterdam Avenue in Manhattan. He weighed 7 pounds even. We lived at 139th Street and Riverside Drive in Harlem, right on the Westside highway in the same building with Tupac, Afeni, Mutulu, and Sekyiwa. I remember during the famous blackout in New York City in July 1977, sleeping in my car, pregnant and unable to walk up those 20-something flights of stairs.

Tupac was always by Yaki's side from the day he was born, eager and proud. Thank goodness I had my lil' Polaroid camera! Yaki was born with a full head of hair which I expected because I always felt a lump in my chest during pregnancy.

Sekyiwa (Tupac's younger half-sister) and Tupac doted over Yaki. From 1971 until Yaki was born in 1977, they were the only children in my life so when Yaki was born it was as if Sekyiwa and Tupac were constantly celebrating his life and wanted to show him the same special love I showed to them. Yaki believed in his heart they were his siblings from the day he was born.

All the kids wanted to look out for Yaki because the was such a good little baby. But more than any of the other children, Sekyiwa was very protective of Yaki. She always wanted to be near him and tend to his needs. As a toddler, Yaki carried around a security blanket. When he cried, Sekyiwa always ran to get it for him. His murder more than 20 years ago affected her deeply and significantly.

When Yaki outgrew the wood cradle, we passed it on to the Asma Abdul Majid family. Asma and her family lived in the Bronx off Gun Hill Road in a huge house with plenty of children. I know it was a source of comfort and joy for many newborns as they navigated their brand-new world. Over the years, their home hosted many of the children's birthday parties and sustained us with love and warmth through the dark days. RIP Umi and Zubiar.

(above) Pac always wanted to hold Yaki so I propped up a big pillow to take this shot. Check out all that hair on Yaki!! Tupac enjoyed mugging for the camera. His smile was infectious!

(opposite) My father holding Yaki next to the wooden crib carved originally for Tupac.

These photos are from the double birthday party for Yaki (born Oct 9) and Sekyiwa (born Oct 3) held at the home of the Abdul Majid family, Bronx.

(left) Mai Ling Cox, Alif Abdul Majid, Tupac.

(right) clockwise from left: Muhammad, Tupac, James, Alif, Tharifa, Kenny, and Nura Hasna eagerly awaiting birthday cake.

(bottom) Kenny Lesane, Nura, Sekyiwa, Yaki (channeling the birthday cake god), Mai Ling.

(opposite top) Nura, Sekyiwa, Yaki, Mai Ling.

(opposite bottom) Loving arms of Umi Asma lighting candles, Muhammad, Tupac, James, Alif, back of Yaki's head.

(top left) Katari Cox aka Kastro

(top right) Yaki and Sekyiwa

(bottom; clockwise from top left) Zubiar, Mutulu, Sekyiwa, Nura, and baby Asha.

(opposite) Sekyiwa

(left) I never could get Yaki to suck on another finger. It always had to be that middle finger!! Even as he grew up, I was always amazed how often he would throw up that one finger. I truly believe it was a source of comfort to him and took him back to these days of baby strollers and being carried everywhere. ca '78.

(below) Yaki with middle finger, ca '90.

(opposite) Katari, Yaki and Tupac. We were in Chinatown, NYC. Tupac with his hands out explaining the world, Yaki with his hands out receiving the knowledge. Tupac was explaining to Yaki why the chickens were in the cages.

When I was young, my mother had exposed me to the great culture of New York City and I was determined to give the children a piece of the Apple, too, so I was always taking the kids somewhere. During those early years with Pac, Sekyiwa, and Yaki, New York City was our playground with its wealth of museums, parks, street festivals, and shows. Tupac loved New York as did I and I really think this exposure helped formulate has master plan how to reshape the world and make it a better place.

In spite of our struggles marked by continued court cases and challenges with the powers that be, the children enjoyed a unique and rewarding life. We went everywhere: the beach, the amusement park, everywhere in NYC, and to New Jersey to visit my family. It was important to get them out of the city to breathe fresh air.

During their games, Tupac was always the director, the one to stage the play. If the children were playing cops and robbers, he decided who was the cop and who was the robber. Tupac assigned the roles and decided who stood where, who spoke first, who got shot first, who fell first, who screamed first, who ran first, who got caught first. The children reveled in his brilliance. Yaki quite simply adored him.

I think the children thought of me as some kind of fairy godmother because I always had a car, always had food in the refrigerator, and was always ready to take them somewhere. I do believe all the exposure to New York's vast cultural delights had an impact on both Yaki and Tupac at an early age. They were always open and creative, resilient yet like sponges as they absorbed all of the city's glory, seemingly impervious to the struggles going on in their midst. In spite of our best efforts to shield them from the anguish and angst of the streets around them, they were still internalizing every moment, good or bad.

(top left and right) Tupac and James Calhoun at Rye Amusement Park

(below) The sheer ecstasy is all over both Katari and Yaki's faces! Nothing made them happier than hanging out with Tupac who could extract such intense joy just from a swing. Tupac had the capacity to immerse himself totally in the business at hand, whether it was play or work... he was so enthralled with life and brought an abundance of joy and energy to every aspect of our lives. He brightened the lives of all who came in contact with him. Park on West Side Highway, NYC.

(opposite top) Yaki and Katari (Kastro) in the hallway of Katari's apartment on 7th Avenue, Harlem.
(opposite bottom) Sekyiwa and Yaki at Rye Playland in New York, '80.
(above) Tupac and Yaki at Rye Amusement Park

CIRCLE OF WOMEN

The real-life soldiers who wove the web of love around Tupac and Yaki were women. They came from many religious, ethnic, and culturally diverse backgrounds. These women marched outside courthouses, at the offices of slumlords, and when we filed lawsuits in federal court to challenge prison conditions. All of these women were dedicated to the fight for the dignity of all people. The seeds of respect and admiration for women were planted at a very early age.

During the Panther 21 trial, Afeni was imprisoned at the Women's House of Detention in Greenwich Village, NYC, located on 6th Avenue and Christopher Street. The House of "D" was built in 1932 and finally demolished in 1974. During its dark history, it housed Ethel Rosenberg, Mae West, and Angela Davis among others. It was an imposing and massive structure. During Afeni's incarceration, we would march outside the prison's looming concrete walls which reminded me of a dungeon. There was always plenty of traffic, noise, and press. Finally, Afeni made bail through the generosity of many church and community organizations. But Afeni's bail was revoked five months into her pregnancy when her co-defendants, Dhoruba Moore and Cetewayo Tabor, did not show up to court.

Returning to the jail posed a dangerous threat to both Afeni and her unborn baby Tupac. The House of D was notorious for its deplorable conditions. It was filthy and unforgiving to the needs of women, especially those with child. The women could holler out the windows down to us in the street and we could holler back up to them. When they hollered down from the top floors "How Long? How Long?", we yelled back up from our protest line, "Not Long! Not Long!"

They would holler for money, for court information, and with phone numbers to call family. We marched around the front and sides of the building where the women could catcall easiest. We were protesting Afeni's bail revocation and demanding proper nutrition for her unborn baby.

It is a miracle Tupac survived and was born strong and healthy. This is why I understood his mercurial disposition as we passed him from lap to lap. Against all odds, he survived the bad food, the unsanitary prison conditions, the trial, the betrayals, and all the tears and rage. Such righteous indignation burned in Tupac like a flame and those of us who were there understood he had every right to be furious.

Each of these women had a profound impact on Tupac's sacred devotion to women. He relished the hugs as there were always women in his life—strong women—whether at work, celebrations, rallies, kitchen dinners, or court. Women held his little hand and illuminated his soul as they stood up for the rights of all people. The spark that lit and fueled his fires came from the women in his early years who simply adored him. Truth and love were his guiding lights under the watchful eyes of many amazing women. Two of the lessons of empowerment Tupac learned as a youngster from the women in his life:

1. Truth is a powerful weapon and can never be defeated.
2. The courts are supposed to enforce laws on one level,
but the ultimate responsibility to challenge injustice belongs to the people.

Crooksie

Carol Jean Crooks was her full name but we called her Crooksie and she was Tupac's godmother. Crooksie was a well-known street hustler in the Jewish-Italian organized crime syndicate, earning a reputation uptown with the Frank Lucas drug organization. She, along with the other women at the House of D (seen below), took care of Afeni during her incarceration. Among the many things they did was iron and starch Afeni's clothes so she would appear presentable and professional in court. That was very important to Crooksie. She made sure every morning a contingent of women sent Afeni to court freshly groomed and looking sharp, her clothing clean, crisp, and fashionable. Crooksie understood Afeni was not just fighting for her life and Tupac's, but for the dignity of all black people, especially the women at The House of D.

Crooksie was the first woman to hold baby Tupac on June 16, 1971, in the delivery room. She was the first woman to whisper in Tupac's ear when he was born. In the delivery room, as the nurse was passing the newborn Tupac to Afeni, she told the nurse to pass him to Crooksie. Crooksie is who named him Parish Crooks. For the first two years of Tupac's life, Crooksie, a hustler from the streets of Brooklyn, protected both Afeni and Tupac at a time when political rivalries between the East Coast Black Panthers and West Coast Black Panthers, instigated by the FBI's COINTELPRO, resulted in shootouts and deaths of many young men and women. In the upcoming documentary *Circle of Women*, Crooksie recounts protecting Afeni after the acquittal. She states, "...after the trial when Afeni came home, she was nervous, but we secured her, and nobody could do anything to her." Truth!

In 1972, Crooksie was arrested and convicted of manslaughter then sentenced to fifteen to life at Bedford Hills. Conditions at the only women's prison in the State of New York were as deplorable as those at the House of D. During her incarceration, Crooksie was instrumental in organizing women to challenge prison conditions but at great cost to her own self.

In August 1974, the women incarcerated at Bedford Hills Correctional Facility rebelled after male jailers severely beat Crooksie. With the other women, Crooksie led the resistance movement against the repressive conditions of Bedford Hills. She was always a voice for the

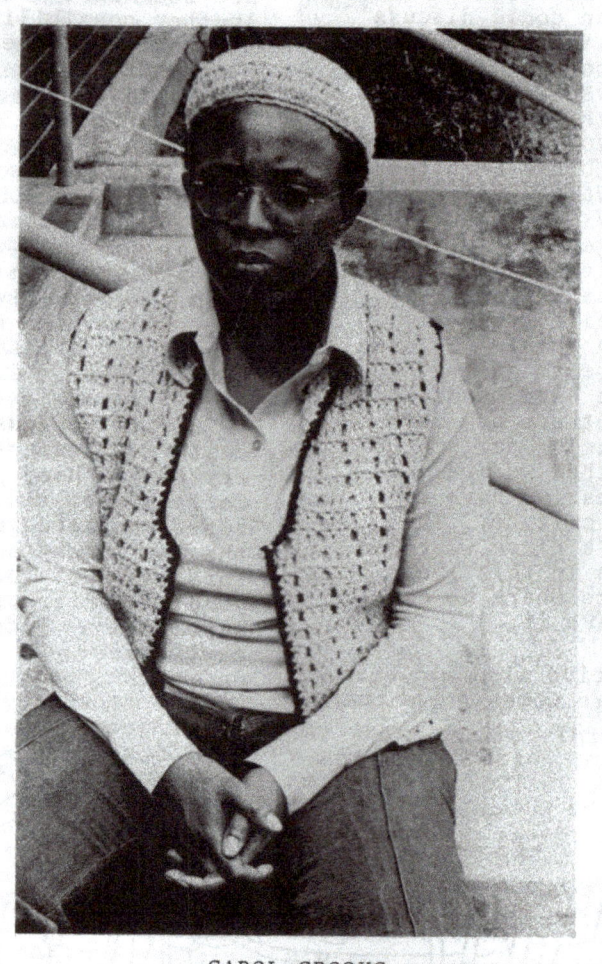

Floating Foundation of Photgraphy

CAROL CROOKS

women. Crooksie reached out to Afeni for help from the Bronx Legal Services where Afeni and I worked. However, we were initially met with resistance from BLS because under the Nixon administration, the government-funded Legal Services offices throughout New York were constantly under threat of de-funding because there were too many poor people withholding rent against slumlords and too many complaints against the corporate entities in violation of human rights.

Regardless, Bronx Legal Services filed several class action lawsuits in federal court in the Southern District on behalf of the women at Bedford Hills. During the lawsuit, the women in the lawsuit were transported to Rikers Island to testify in federal court about the conditions at Bedford Hills and denial of due process rights during disciplinary proceedings. It was here their paths crossed with Assata Shakur, another woman who symbolized strength and courage to young Tupac.

Eventually we prevailed, even winning some financial restitution for the women in the ruling from Powell v. Ward. The women used the money to purchase computers and sponsor family day events. Tupac was only a toddler but so full of life, wandering off and getting lost in the prison during one of the family day events at Bedford Hills. We laughed so hard about that.

When Crooksie finally came home, she always tried to stay in contact with Tupac when they lived in Harlem. Everyone knew she was Tupac's godmother. She would have him come every Friday to her house to get some money and see what he was up to.

Later as his career took flight during filming of *Above the Rim*, Crooksie tried to get a message to him about rumors she was hearing. Always with her ears in the streets, she was being warned about his associations and careless behavior. Keeping up with Tupac during these days in 1993 was difficult, especially for people who loved him so. I am convinced she was one of the few people who could have wrapped that veil of protection over him once again, just like she did the day he was born if only she could have caught up with him as he darted forward faster and higher facing more peril than we had ever imagined.

Carol Jean Crooks was an intuitive survivor of a patriarchal system that demeans and oppresses women. Crooksie was a force to be reckoned with in the women's prison rights movement.

She was one of the real unsung heroes of Tupac's life who will forever be in my heart—strong, courageous, fearless, vulnerable, and without fail, she loved her some Tupac.

Assata Shakur

Afeni and I were both on the board of directors of the National Task Force for COINTELPRO Litigation and Research (NTFCLR). Assata, like so many other student organizers, became a target of the FBI's counterintelligence program. Many fled for their lives or were incarcerated after being falsely charged with crimes to "neutralize" and "disrupt" their work. When Assata was captured May 2, 1973, during a shootout on the NJ Turnpike, Assata had been either wanted for questioning or indicted in eleven separate incidents. She was found either not guilty, a mistrial declared, or charges dismissed in each one. Afeni sat at the defense table along with Assata and her attorney Stanley Cohen to assist in her defense. Afeni was a brilliant strategist, having successfully represented herself during the New York Panther 21 trial. In 1975, Senator Frank Church's committee released their investigation of the FBI's secret plan called COINTELPRO. From the Church report, we learned evidence was fabricated against innocent people who were rigorously prosecuted by state and local agencies. Exposing the conspiracy of COINTELPRO against Panthers was central to mounting a defense. Throughout the trial, we sat in the front row of the courtroom so Tupac could witness the power of women confronting injustice and winning. He was so well behaved, this time observing from the courtroom pews and not as a fetus curled up in his mother's belly. Assata was acquitted for these Queens bank robbery charges on January 16, 1976.

Yuri Kochiyama

Yuri Kochiyama was a renowned activist and human rights organizer who worked with Malcolm X. Our struggles for human rights were one as we marched side by side with the children in tow. Tupac knew these women personally and they knew him. We would meet at Yuri's small Harlem apartment to strategize for upcoming rallies and events. Tupac learned from her about the ravages of nuclear war on the people of Nagasaki and Hiroshima, the Japanese concentration camps here in America, and the interconnectedness of all our struggles. A staunch advocate for human rights, Yuri graced our lives with love and conviction. We were woven into each other's lives, working and living together to create a better world.

Flo Kennedy

The audacity of the women who surrounded the young Tupac had a profound impact on his formative years. These were courageous women who pioneered change by challenging unjust laws and practices, often at significant cost to their personal lives.

None were gutsier and more fearless than the bold Florynce Kennedy. Flo was a notorious feminist, civil rights advocate, lawyer, and consummate thorn in the side of the halls of injustice. Though departing from the politics of her white feminist movement sisters, Flo insisted all movements were bound together by the same white supremacist patriarchy that oppressed everyone. It was her determination to bind all movements together and she was the bridge connecting the liberation for black justice with the white feminist elite.

Flo organized fund raisers and boycotts for Angela Davis and the Soledad Brothers. She represented H. Rap Brown (Jalil El Amin). During the Panther 21 trial, Flo would stage invasions of vacation enclaves at Fire Island, New York, an elite exclusive vacation spot where she had a home. During these demonstrations she invited lawyers for and members of the BPP. One of her demands was that the Fire Island dining halls place "gefilte fish, ham hocks, and greens" on the same menu. What a woman!

Flo was on the board of directors for National Task Force for Cointelpro Litigation and Research. Going up against white patriarchy politics was nothing new to her, whether it was the FBI, the New York State Supreme Court, or Harvard University. It was all the same. We met with her frequently in her home on Fire Island with Afeni and baby Tupac. Flo held Afeni in high regard after the New York Panther 21 court victory and she especially relished Tupac, having worked tirelessly for their freedom during the trial.

After Assata's deadlocked jury verdict in the Bronx Bank Robbery trial in 1973, the judge ordered the new trial to begin the next day, an unprecedented demand. Evelyn Williams, Assata's aunt and lawyer, withdrew from the case. Flo became counsel of record with Assata as co-counsel.

Flo was concerned as she hadn't tried a case in court in many years. We assured her what Assata needed was not so much a brilliant trial attorney, but rather a loud mouth, unafraid, and an impertinent defender of human rights. We worked closely with Flo during the trial. Tupac sat with us every day in the courtroom observing Flo cross examine witnesses, in search of the truth, probing, objecting, always standing tall. He was a mere two years old, yet as always, attentive and eager, taking it all in.

In December 1973, the jury found Assata not guilty. We celebrated at Flo's home on Fire Island. Tupac was the smallest and youngest guest present with his starry eyes ablaze with wonderment. Surrounded by the most outrageously raucous women of the times, these moments became building blocks of his consciousness perfectly placed.

Vivian Smith

Tupac came with me to visit my mother, Vivian, in New Jersey on many occasions. My mother would play classical Beethoven sonatas and Duke Ellington on the piano along with show tunes from Rogers & Hammerstein. Tupac would sit on the piano bench with her and finger the ivory keys. He was spellbound by the sound, almost in a trance as my mother's hands moved rhythmically over the keys. My mother adored him.

Delia H. Martin

When I would bring Tupac to East Orange as a little boy, Delia, my grandmother, was one of the women who would hug him, feed him, and read to him. There were always Ebony magazines, the NAACP Crisis magazine, and great political conversations at the dinner table for him to absorb. It was the early 70s and the nation was still reeling from riots, Martin Luther King's assassination, and the country was in turmoil. Tupac sat with his big eyes taking in this assemblage of extended family, all who knew his story of survival. She spoke to him about all the heroes. Paul Robeson was her favorite as she had worked on his case when the US government was persecuting him for his courageous stand for human rights. This was before Yaki was born. I am so grateful Tupac had the opportunity to be in the presence of my dear Nana and my mother.

Yaki's great-grandmother Delia with then-New Jersey Governor Keane in Trenton, overseeing his signing of a proclamation marking February as Black History Month.

Kidada Jones

Tupac was accustomed to women who were forces of nature. He had been in their company all his life. Women who were in perpetual motion, capable of surviving through the harshest of times emerging unscathed. Kidada Jones was the tempest to Tupac's torrential windstorm, one whose winds blew him into unchartered territory because for once he had met his match. His days of philandering were coming to an end. This girlfriend, now his fiancée, was not like the others. She is the daughter of Quincy Jones and accustomed to genius talent and late night studio sessions creating musical magic. By the age of 21, she already was entrenched in her own career as a designer for Tommy Hilfiger. Her sister Rashida gave Tupac a lesson in humility and grace when she penned the letter criticizing him for his off-handed comments about Quincy. Her brother is QD3, a producer and talent in his own right. Her mother is the late Peggy Lipton, so her beauty was inherently adorned. She is the granddaughter of the late Sarah Jones, a force of nature who took no tea for the fever. This was the type of woman Tupac was accustomed to all his life: women who stood up for what they believed, unabashedly intolerant of disrespect, and prepared to step to you without hesitation. Tupac apologized to Quincy and gained a newfound respect for the Jones clan.

Kidada had her head on straight and looked down on all the female debauchery in his circle. She commanded and demanded respect. Tupac loved and admired her independence when they first met in NYC. He could not pretend with Kidada. She was the real deal and he knew it. He wanted to keep her close during his "transformation" but needed a little time to save face with the homies. Yes, he was falling in love, and yes, marriage was on the horizon. It was time to grow up. Time to step up and allow real love to flourish and renew his soul.

But as he tried to get right, he made missteps and would call me so I could call "K" and try and smooth things over. Haha! My response was, "Pac, you messed up. She's not having it. If you don't grow up, you're gonna lose this one." Tupac had a habit of twisting his mouth, nervously chewing, whenever he was stressed. He couldn't fool me. I knew he really was enamored by Kidada. He just needed more time to grow.

After the death of Tupac and Yaki, I was in a whirlwind of devastation, just roaming around numb to the world. Quincy called me to come work for him, at the prodding of Kidada. This was May 1997. Working for Quincy was like easing on down that yellow brick road every day–magical. So full of wonderment at his lifetime achievements, his decades of musical genius, the mountain of love he poured into my soul that healed the holes in my heart.

The gratitude and respect I have for this family is both profound and knows no bounds. I think of what could have been with Kidada and Tupac–the beautiful family they would be raising. Heartbreaking.

When I found out Yaki had two girls, they were already three years old. Kidada was the first person I called. Words cannot describe the pure elation and joy in her voice!! All was not lost. We now had two beautiful girls of Yaki's to embrace. Despite all her losses—Aaliyah, MJ, Tupac—and the profound pain and overwhelming grief, Kidada has taught me much about courage. Courage on the battlefield is one thing. Courage at the loss of loved ones requires a different inner resolve, guts, defiance, and strong connection to spirit.

Nothing but love and respect to this woman who kept me spiritually grounded with her compassion, love and inner strength. Indeed, my dear Kidada, life is eternal.

(top) Kidada with Yaki's daughters, ca 2001.
(opposite left) Kidada and Tupac. Kidada loved to put these little messages on their photos. Italy, ca '95.
(bottom left) Peggy and Nyasia at Hollywood Bowl, ca 2013.

Peggy Lipton Jones

Kidada's mom, Peggy, transcended categorization. As an actress, she exuded warmth and beauty on screen from the popular 60s-era TV series *Mod Squad* to her final film in 2017, *A Dog's Purpose*. Our friendship was filled with such joy and good times, her light always shining, prodding us forward with love to be our best. Totally devoted to her daughters, Kidada and Rashida, this was a woman whose spirit of kindness blessed all who came in contact with her. She simply adored my granddaughters and they adored her. There will never be another mortal in my lifetime whose pure essence of love and grace touched my soul so deeply. One of the many blessings of this journey, to have been a witness to her glory.

BILLY GARLAND — *Redemption*

*The day misspent,
the love misplaced,
has inside it
the seed of redemption.
Nothing is exempt
from resurrection.
~ Kay Ryan*

During my college years at Northern Michigan University starting in 1967, the country had erupted in civil disobedience as students demanded an end to the Vietnam War. Many of us were still reeling from the assassination of Malcolm X in 1965 and then we were hit with the assassination of Martin Luther King in 1968. During these turbulent times, the Black Panther Party was founded. It upheld the principle of service to the community that was suffering from inadequate health care, improper nutrition, inferior schools, and unfit housing. In 1970, I joined their protests outside the courthouse at 100 Centre Street demanding justice for the NY Panther 21 defendants. Soon thereafter, I transferred to the Brooklyn campus of Long Island University to be closer to the action, the protests, and student activism in New York City.

Afeni met William "Billy" Garland, Tupac's biological father, in New Jersey when she stayed with us to get away from the chaos of the trial. Tupac was born just a little over a month after the Panther 21 were acquitted of all charges. When Tupac was born, Afeni was married to Lumumba Shakur and Billy had a family with his wife Carol.

Afeni felt vulnerable, having just given birth to Tupac and now witnessing Panthers being shot down in the street by other Panthers. She became the poster child for so many movements that were eager to exploit and capitalize on the courage she showed during the Panther 21 trial. We posted security for Tupac and Afeni constantly, as Afeni shuffled the baby between a friend's home in the Village to our "Panther Pad" in East Orange with Solomon Thomas and Cheryl Davila.

We took turns watching out so she

could sleep. There was always a circle of women who passed Tupac from lap to lap, lavishing him with kisses and adoration. There was no doubt he was special—he survived. She knew when she came to NJ that she and Tupac were protected and loved. Baby Tupac thrived, enjoying the arms of many who loved him dearly, including his father Billy, who had three other children. During this time, I would bring the baby for overnights with Billy and his siblings.

As Billy and Afeni attempted to negotiate a future for Pac, their personal family struggle was quickly overshadowed by fires of rebellion burning in America. The Panthers were demonized by the media, which brewed an atmosphere of mistrust and division between the East Coast and West Coast BPP groups. The media's negative portrayal of the BPP was seeded by the FBI and was later exposed by the Frank Church Committee investigating these FBI abuses and their campaign to neutralize the BPP. There was a palpable tension as great people fought for human rights to save the soul of America, only to lose theirs in the process. (Ironically, another East Coast/West Coast rivalry would explode 20 years later with Tupac in the middle.) The division of parental responsibilities was muddied by the tumultuous reality of the early 70s East Coast/West Coast violence. Everyone was in survival mode as the external war against the BPP instigated by COINTELPRO was effectively destroying the organization internally and people were literally dying. There was no time for relationships to grow or to work through disagreements, much less raise a love child. Decisions were made that did not take into account what was best for Tupac. Sadly, as is always the case in these situations, those hastily-made choices had a significant impact on his life in the years to come.

After the Quad Studio shooting, Billy was at the hospital and was at Tupac's bedside when he woke up. It was at that point they began to resurrect their relationship.

(left) Billy Garland, Newark, NJ, 2018.

(above) Billy and Tupac. Illustration by Ronald "Riskie Forever" Brent.

Bronx Legal Services -
Serving the People

Located at 579 Courtlandt Avenue, Bronx Legal Services was home base for our organizing work in the community as well as where we raised our children. Between 1972 and 1981, Afeni and I worked as paralegals at Bronx Legal Services (BLS), organizing tenants living in deplorable conditions. At first, Afeni could not start working in 1972 because she was in a very bad car accident. I started in her place and held down her job until she recovered. After her recovery, another paralegal position became available, and the managing attorney Richard Fischbein hired me.

We operated under the Community Action for Legal Services (CALS), federally funded by the Legal Services Corporation Act. With this funding structure, BLS was only allowed to represent civil cases. In poor neighborhoods like ours, this involved evictions first and foremost, then all kinds of administrative hearings for grievances regarding welfare, unemployment, Medicaid, and Social Security. We were always underfunded and constantly under scrutiny if we dared to expose too many housing code violations or forced too many court-ordered building inspections. The city-wide negligence of these impoverished communities was so vast and so encompassing that we were always spearheading new areas of law in response to the needs of the people. Even though we would stop an eviction, there were still had the underlying issues to address—health problems, drug addiction, mis-education, and poverty. It was a cycle of endless despair.

Despite the destruction of the BPP by the FBI and State forces, the true mission of the BPP continued with the same people and the same attorneys. Richard Fischbein worked with many community organizations prior to becoming the managing attorney at BLS. When he became the head at BLS, he hired us. In our work at BLS, we encouraged and educated tenants on how to take control of their lives and their buildings when slumlords abandoned them or refused to provide basic services, like heat and running water. This was a continuation of the work done on so many levels in the BPP, particularly the advocacy for the right to decent housing, which was one of the points of The Black Panther Party for Self-Defense Ten-Point Platform and Program.

Many of the tenants we helped through BLS were residents of the very same buildings we organized during the BPP days… but now we were getting paid to organize and advocate! In the 70s, the Bronx was burning. The slumlords were burning their buildings or simply abandoning them. It was a wasteland of urban renewal displacement and redlining discrimination. We helped the people reclaim their humanity by setting up non-profits to rehab their abandoned buildings. On a national scale, President Richard Nixon and members of Congress were heavily pressured to de-fund the Legal Services Corporation by the slumlords whose buildings we were organizing into rent strikes. However, Congress and the rest of the elected officials actually did the just and right thing by continuing to fund the Legal Services Center.

You cannot beg for freedom. You must demand it.

Through Bronx Legal Services, we took all of our organizing skills that we refined during our time with the BPP and we continued to do the core work of the party, which was to provide basic services and care to the people while teaching them empowerment skills to make it happen for themselves. That service to the people was always the purpose of the BPP. It was this core ethic of caring for the people and empowering them that Tupac embraced as a youngster and carried through his whole life.

We pooled our money together and bought a mimeograph machine, which is essentially a printing press. We wrote and printed our own leaflets, notices, and pamphlets with information for the community about the laws and their rights as tenants. The mimeograph had automatic and manual options. Tupac loved to flip the switch on the machine to put it on manual so he could be the one to ink the plates, turn the wheel, and watch as the pages churned out in colors. He was so little back then that he had to stand on a chair to reach the wheel!

BLACK PANTHER PARTY 10-POINT PROGRAM

1. We want freedom. We want power to determine the destiny of our black community.
2. We want full employment for our people.
3. We want an end to the robbery by the white man of our black community.
4. We want decent housing, fit for shelter of human beings.
5. We want education for our people that exposes the true nature of this decadent American society. We want education that teaches us our true history and our role in the present day society.
6. We want all black men to be exempt from military service.
7. We want an immediate end to police brutality and murder of black people.
8. We want freedom for all black men held in federal, state, county and city prisons and jails.
9. We want all black people when brought to trial to be tried in court by a jury of their peer group or people from their black communities, as defined by the constitution of the United States.
10. We want land, bread, housing, education, clothing, justice and peace, and as our major political objective, a United Nations-supervised plebiscite to be held throughout the black colony in which only black colonial subjects will be allowed to participate, for the purpose of determining the will of black people as to their national destiny.

Black Child's Pledge

I pledge allegiance to my Black people.

I pledge to develop my mind and body to the greatest extent possible.

I will learn all that I can in order to give my best to my people in their struggle for liberation.

I will keep myself physically fit, building a strong body free from drugs and other substances that weaken me and make me less capable of protecting myself, my family, and my Black brothers and sisters.

I will unselfishly share my knowledge and understanding with them in order to bring about change more quickly.

I will discipline myself to direct my energies thoughtfully and constructively rather than wasting them in idle hatred.

I will train myself never to hurt or allow others to harm my Black brothers and sisters for I recognize that we need every Black man, woman, and child to be physically, mentally and psychologically strong.

These principles I pledge to practice daily and to teach them to others in order to unite my people.

THE FIGHT AGAINST SLUMLORDS

To be a landlord in the city of New York is to be associated with one of the most vicious and avaricious vampires of the land. These misery mongerers are the banking / real-estate interests who not only run New York, but ran and eventually bought the Mayoralty for Abraham Beame. They are of various criminal types, including but certainly not limited to judges, lawyers, stockbrokers, Bronx Board of Realtors, Real Estate Board of New York, National Association of Realtors, not to even mention the Council of Property Owners Association and the American Property Rights Association. Their claim to the land is known in international law as the "bandit rule" and says that "when a people steal land and occupy it for a long time, the world will recognize that land as belonging to them", which is how the u.s. claims amerikkka and the landlords claim the rat-traps Black people live in as well as the destinies of our children.

For those of us who see the struggle for independent land as inseperable from our struggle for freedom, it is more than apparant that landlords/real-estate are consciously using "bandit rule' to restrain/exploit our most precious resource.....our people. Landlords carry out their genocidal plan by forcing the people to live with rats, roaches, vermin infestation, no heat or hot water in the winter, fires due to faulty electrical wiring, lead-poisoning to our young and exorbitant rents. Tenants who organize rent strikes against such inhumane living conditions are intimidated, harrassed and brutalized by landlord/goon squads - the cutting off of services (heat, running water, lights) is a common practice of landlords desperately attempting to break the rent strike.

Essentially the tenant has strategically elevated himself into a powerful position through economic pressure upon the landlord by giving the rent to the Tenant's Association and not the landlord. Thusly, the landlord/bandit is forced into re-evaluating his previous posture of blood-sucking our people, our homes and OUR LAND.

Africans in Amerikkka, as tenants, have sub-consciously engaged in strategic struggle for land. In affirming their humanity, they have unwittingly embraced the "civilized rule of land possession". What this means is that our people have historically lived on this land for 300 years. We have worked to develop this land, paid for the land with our rent monies, fought terror and night riders/goon squads to stay there......and that land is unmistakenly ours. This is known as the principled rule of international law that gives Black folk their claim for land in Amerikkka. It is the law that opposes "bandit rule" and the only law whereby Black people as tenants will be able to live their lives in peace and brotherhood.

FREE THE LAND

We pooled our money together, purchased a mimeograph machine, and published our own community notices, leaflets, and articles. Above is a page from one of our first publications "Take the Land", Vol. 1, No. 1, 1973.

(opposite) Tupac printed out this Creed on the mimeograph machine constantly and shared it with everyone he met. He carried the Creed in his heart to the grave. Written by Shirley Williams, The Black Panther, October 26, 1968.

Those who survived the dismantling of revolutionary and activist organizations continued building a resistance movement and Tupac was on the front lines of the struggle in the 70s and 80s. He traveled with us to the prison in Bedford Hills on family day events when we would visit the plaintiffs we were representing in federal court. He was by our side at meetings in the South Bronx with tenants organizing rent strikes against the slumlords through our jobs at Bronx Legal Services. The strategy was not just to withhold rent due to uninhabitable living conditions but to escrow the money into the bank to encourage not just protest, but ownership of the building. Self-determination at work.

We were soon contacted by Tupac's godmother Crooksie who was then incarcerated at Bedford Hills Correctional Institution. Afeni and I expanded the Prisoners' Rights department at BLS to also protect female prisoners. We filed several lawsuits in federal court challenging the conditions at Bedford Hills. Additionally, we filed a lawsuit against Eastern Correctional Facility in Napanoch, NY, on behalf of Frank Abney. The federal case was Abney v. Ku Klux Klan. Many of the correctional guards at the state prisons were open members of the Ku Klux Klan.

A lot of good people collaborated and joined forces to make concrete differences. We had a great team and made plenty of case law that had a profound and lasting impact both in the community of the South Bronx and in the State of New York.

The children were a permanent fixture at the legal offices where we worked. Tupac, Sekyiwa, and Yaki came with us to the South Bronx offices on Courtlandt Avenue. They practically grew up there in playpens as we interviewed clients and drafted Order to Show Cause documents to stop illegal evictions. Tupac learned firsthand the psychological warfare African Americans suffered from substandard housing, substandard education, drug abuse, and economic starvation. He observed the battle we waged daily in service to the people, just as we had done in the BPP.

It was during these years that Tupac learned the power of the people's movements. Our strong Legal Services Union (NOLSW) taught him the importance of labor movements, whose roots were embedded in New York City history. Our work with prisoners taught Tupac the injustice of mass incarceration but the empowerment that came with a strong prisoners' rights movement. Our work at Lincoln Hospital showed Tupac how drugs were used as a weapon against the people to pacify and destroy the minds and bodies of entire communities.

In 1979-80, our union (NOLSW) traveled to Tupelo, Mississippi, to support the Mississippi Rural Legal Services—headed by the renowned civil rights lawyer Lewis Myers, Jr.—in their fight against local right-wing elements and the Ku Klux Klan.

By the time Tupac joined the hip hop scene, he already knew the organizing potential of hip hop as a movement. His voice was always a means to an end and that end was a people's movement for justice and reform using music to stimulate and motivate the young people. Always the visionary, he was miles ahead of the cultural materialism and hedonism that dominates the genre today. Bronx Legal Services was a bastion of justice in his young mind. He carried these tenets with him throughout his life. He also knew that the laws in America were used to institutionalize racism and our movement must challenge these unjust laws and empower the people in the process. He witnessed on a regular basis how organization and mobilization worked hand in hand.

But most importantly, he learned you cannot beg for freedom. You must demand it. This was his mantra, this was his plan. Tupac executed this plan every day of his life.

He just needed more time.

UNITED STATES DISTRICT COURT
SOUTHERN DISTRICT OF NEW YORK

FRANK ABNEY, et. al.,

    Plaintifss,   75 Civ. 1026 (D.B.B.)

 -against-

INDEPENDENT NORTHERN KLAN, INC., et. al., NOTICE TO PRODUCE DOCUMENTS

    Defendants.

 PLEASE TAKE NOTICE, that pursuant to F.R.C.P., §34, the Defendants are required to produce at the offices of Community Action for Legal Services, 335 Broadway, New York, N.Y., on September 9, 1977 at 10:00 A.M., the following documents for inspection and copying:

 1. The Inspector General's Investigation File and report mentioned in Louis Douglas' deposition taken March 10, 1977.

 2. Any and all documents pertaining to or related to any investigation of Klu Klux Klan at any New York State correctional facility.

        Yours, etc.,

        EMILIO P. GAUTIER, ESQ.,
        Project Director
        BRONX LEGAL SERVICES, CORP. C.
        579 Courtlandt Avenue
        Bronx, New York 10451
        Tel. 212-993-6250
        STEPHEN M. LATIMER, Of Counsel
        Attorneys for Plaintiffs

MIDNIGHT SPECIAL

Prisoners News

DARE TO STRUGGLE DARE TO WIN

Midnight Special
853 Broadway
New York, New York 10003

February 1977   Vol. 5, #10

FREE FRANK DOTTON

Since the days of slavery, Black men have been framed, imprisoned and often executed after being charged with rape of white women. Throughout the South, Blackmen were sometimes murdered for supposedly looking at a white woman. Today the rape frame-up charge is used against Third World men as a continuing process of oppression of our communities.

"My Name is Frank Dotton. I live in Jamaica, Queens. In 1974, I was busy doing odd jobs as a handy-man. On May 13, 1974, after painting and repairing my wife's car, I decided to get some gas. My woman was in her ninth month of pregnancy and she could go into labor at anytime. While on Jamaica line, two plain-clothes detectives in an unmarked car pulled our car over. They said the car I was driving resembled the description given to them by a complainant and that I should go to the precinct so that they could ask me some questions.

While at the police station, I was questioned and viewed by at least seven different women, given two summons and photographed. I was threatened by Detective Barlollotte. He said that he would get me one way or the other. The car was impounded and I was set free. On Friday, May 17, 1974, four days after they had first stopped me, they came back this time to arrest me. I was charged with rape, robbery, sodomy, and kidnapping. The kidnapping charge was dropped before I even went to court. The robbery trial was dismissed for lack of evidence. Justice Agresta was biased and prejudiced from the beginning."

Assistant D.A. Michael Swead insisted on convicting Frnak Dotton to further his political career. The constitution guarantees a person trial by jury of his peers. Frank Dotton was tried by an all white middle age jury and not by people from his community.

The alleged victim was not sure about anything from the beginning. She changed her story two or three times from the Grand Jury to the conclusion of the trial. The police claimed the car that Frank was driving was used in the crime. No evidence was found in that vehicle. The police searched the house where Frank Dotton lived with wife and family. This is the same house where the woman claimed the incident occured. However, there were no fingerprints, weapon, hair, clothes or anything else to substantiate the rape story.

Four witnesses testified and established where Frank Dotton was at the time and date of the alleged incident. Apparently, their testimony was disregarded by the all-white jury. Even with the lack of evidence and his witnesses testimony, he was tried and convicted for a period of seven to twenty-one years.

Frank Dotton, like other Black and Third World men are fighting for freedom and to prove his innocence. This could have happened to anyone in our community. It is all of our responsibility to unify and help to free Frank Dotton, because in doing so we will prevent the same injustice form happening to any one of us. For immediate action: 1) write the Governor kemanding new trial or a full pardon for Frank Dotton 2) send contributions to the Frank Dotton Defense Committee, P.O. Box 32244, Jamaica, N.Y. 11431

FREE FRANK KHALI ABNEY

In 1971 Nixon had come to power under the platform of law and order. The Black Community was under attack. The U.S. government had launched its Cointel program which was exposed during Watergate and which was designed to kill Black Leaders, destroy Black organizations and disrupt the growing political consciousness of the Black Community. On the streets of New York, Black youths were being killed by trigger - happy police. Because of this, the resistence of the Black Community was at a very high level, and the police were frantic to frame-up people to set examples.

Frank Khali Abney was arrested in Brooklyn and charged with attempted murder of a policeman. According to the 2 arresting officers, Khali pointed a gun, one of the officers heard a click, but no shot was fired. Upon arrest, no weapon was found on him.

Khali was defended by Egbert Craig, a Real Estate

lawyer, who persuaded him to waive trial by jury. The case was heard by now-retired Judge Michael Kearn, known throughout Brooklyn as a "Hanging Judge". Khali testified that the police officers accosted him on the street and that he was beaten and dragged into the station before he was informed of the charges against him. After a trial of less than 2 days, and based solely on the contradictory police testimony, Khali was found guilty by Judge Kearn, He was sentenced to 15 years to life. Two appeals on Khali's behalf have been denied. A recent court of appeals decision in a case similar to Khali's has termed Judge Kearn racist and biased.

While in prison at Eastern Correctional Facility at Napanoch, N.Y., Khali founded and is the President of the Eastern Branch of the NAACP. Khali has led the struggle against the racist oppression of the Ku Klux Klan in New York's prison system. He is a plaintiff along with the NAACP in 2 suits against the KKK. These suits expose the Klan domination in Napanoch and the extent to which Khali and other prisoners have been harassed by the Klan (guards and civilian employees) because they are Black and politically active. Prisoners have been beaten, harassed and fire-bombed in their cells. Even though he has been one of the main victims of such terror tactics, Khali remains a leader in the struggle for prisoners' human rights.

WE DEMAND THAT FRANK KHALI ABNEY BE GIVEN A NEW TRIAL OR GRANTED A FULL PARDON!!!!!!!

What you can do to help:
Khali will only be freed if the people demand Justice. If you want to help, please contact us, The Frank Abney Defense Committee at:
P.O. Box 57, Lefferts St. Station
Brooklyn, New York 11238
These are the ways you can help:
Write to the Governor or your state legislator telling him/her you demand a new trial or pardon for Khali.
Call us for our petitions and help us circulate them.
Invite us to meet you and others in your community.
Put us in touch with other friends and families of prisoners and other defense committees.
"When I go back on trial, I won't be going alone. Justice will be on trial with me. As long as I am allowed to stay in prison, no Black person can feel safe walking the streets of New York."

Frank Khali Abney

Families and Friends of Prisoners Mutual Assistance League

Families and Friends of Prisoners Mutual Assistance League

We are working to develop the concept of the FFPMAL because we see the need to organize people in oppressed Black, Puerto Rican, and poor white communities into a force which can work to transform the judicial and prison systems in this country. We are attempting to develop around the relatives of prisoners who are prepared to struggle and build a network of people who can support each other in behalf of their imprisoned relatives and loved ones. We are seeking to organize people in our communities into a political force which can rectify the injustices and change the judicial and prison systems.

People support each other when they realize that all we have is each other. The basic reason that we are so easily oppressed and exploited by the system is that we are unorganized. Many people think it is possible to find individual solutions to the poverty and problems of our communities. This is not true and never has been true. If there is to be justice for our people then we must organize and initiate the necessary work and demands. Some areas in which the FFPMAL may work are:
1. Doing community outreach to educate others about specific cases of injustices through petitions, leaflets, posters, letters and cards.
2. Setting up contacts in the communities which can be used to investigate situations which might be necessary for a legal defense or appeal.
3. Serving as a base of support for struggles initiated by prisoners around the overall prison conditions.
4. Counseling people about legal assistance, penal procedures how to start a community campaign in behalf of prisoners.
5. Raising funds to continue and expand work.
6. Lobbying and working with legislators who claim to represent our communities.
7. Initiating whatever direct action campaigns (picketing, marches, rallies) which may be necessary to dramatize the injustices and conditions in prisons.

There are many people and skills in our communities which if organized would become an effective force for change and freedom. At this point, FFPMAL is a proposal rather than a concrete reality. We need to hear from the people who are prepared to work to develop this vitally necessary program. Write to:
Midnight Special FFPMAL c/o Attica Now
219 E. 10th Street
New York, N.Y.

Midnight Special was one of the prisoner's rights publications that supported our legal lawsuits on behalf of inmates' rights.

Yaki making phone calls at my desk Bronx Legal Services, 579 Courtlandt Avenue, Bronx, ca. '80.

My mother Vivian Smith (pictured on opposite page) graduated from Lincoln Hospital 1941 and was a visiting home nurse in New York City. I learned my regard for service to the people from her and she learned it from her mother, Delia Martin.

LINCOLN SCHOOL FOR NURSES

on the occasion of its

100ᵀᴴ ANNIVERSARY

invites the public to review the growth in spirit and accomplishment, which has brought "The Society for the Relief of Worthy, Aged, Indigent Colored Persons" of 1839 to its present-day organization and public service.

Lincoln Hospital- *Ground Zero*

Still in operation today, Lincoln Hospital has a rich historical legacy for African Americans. It was established in 1839 by white women of conscience. They founded The Society for the Relief of Worthy Aged Indigent Colored Persons and as such, they opened "The Home for the Colored Aged," (as it was first known) located in a building on 51st Street and the Hudson River. By the late 1890s, it had evolved into a full-fledged hospital for all races and was renamed Lincoln Hospital in honor of President Abraham Lincoln. In 1898, a training school for Negro nurses was opened at Lincoln Hospital and this school was the first of its kind for African American women in the United States. In those days, this country highly restricted the education of African Americans and the Lincoln School for Nurses provided a unique opportunity to women of color who had been refused entrance to the segregated Ivy League institutions.

Availing herself of this opportunity was my mother Vivian Martin Smith. She was the epitome of intellect, character, and beauty. She graduated from Lincoln Hospital in 1941 with her RN degree. This was a time when Blacks were rarely able to attend institutions of higher learning and generally expected to pursue a life as a housemaid or field hand. New Jersey was a segregated bastion of post-slavery Jim Crow. Her acceptance and graduation from the Lincoln School for Nurses was the beginning of my family's involvement in this institution's long tradition of struggle for human rights which has continued since its inception.

It was no coincidence that we returned to Lincoln Hospital in 1974 to start a new program to detox addicts from the devastation of heroin. In solidarity, the BPP and the Young Lords plus many more valiant brothers and sisters fought the drug epidemic of the South Bronx using Lincoln Hospital as ground zero to educate the people.

Lincoln Hospital's acupuncture drug detoxification clinic was founded by activists from the Black Panther Party, The Republic of New Afrika, the Young Lords, and Students for a Democratic Society. This program was developed by Mutulu Shakur and other activists as a direct response to the ravages of drug addiction and the profit-driven pharmaceutical industry. It used both holistic and political education to stop drug trafficking and drug addiction which plagued the South Bronx. It took courage and commitment for Mutulu to become a licensed acupuncturist. He was also the co-founder of the Black Acupuncture Advisory Association of North America (BAAANA) in Harlem. Mutulu was a champion for human rights and was recognized by the People's Republic of China for having detoxed and treated hundreds of

LIBERATION FOR TUPAC WAS ALWAYS ROOTED IN THE SPOKEN WORD. NO EQUIVOCATION – BE DIRECT AND SPEAK THE TRUTH.

patients. We called him Doc. He was a tremendous influence in the community and sacrificed so much in service to the people.

The Lincoln Detox Program was recognized worldwide for its unique approach to treating addiction. Addicts flooded the clinic to break the hold of heroin by using acupuncture instead of methadone. The walls of Lincoln Detox were covered with charts of the human body displaying meridian paths and points associated with every organ of the body. Tupac was around seven years old when he would help the clinicians administer acupressure to patients and would wave the burning Moxa sticks around the room under the watchful eye and tutelage of Mutulu. This effective and drug-free methodology caused pharmaceutical companies such as Eli Lilly to wage warfare against Lincoln Detox Program in an attempt to force the clinic to prescribe and use methadone, not acupuncture, for heroin addicts.

It led to many confrontations with the pharmaceutical industry and the hospital administration. Some, like Dr. Richard Taft, lost their lives for this, the real war on drugs. Through this, we marched, we protested, and we challenged policies that kept people chained to poverty and despair. Of course, Tupac was by our side every step of the way. Lincoln Hospital was our space for organizing the community to demand healthcare that was humane and not dictated by pharmaceutical company interests.

Tupac was filled with energy and exuberance as he went with us to Lincoln Hospital, the community meetings, the prisons, and the offices of BLS. He was such a joy to all who encountered him. He was so proud to give out the leaflets at meetings or even just walking down the street. Even at this early age, he understood we could serve the people by showing them options to drug addiction and we could teach tenants how to fight back against slumlords and that the way to do this was with the power of words. Liberation for Tupac was always rooted in the spoken word. No equivocation—be direct and speak the truth. These were the lessons he learned from his early activism.

Contrary to the mass media misinformation that continues to this very day, the work of the BPP was concerned with the basic day-to-day issues of the people: drug abuse, mass incarceration, landlord/tenant abuses, and health. From early on, the Black Panther Party understood the scourge of drugs in the community was a tool to keep people in a state of poverty and compliance. The BPP considered drug dealers as enemies of the people. As such, these dealers were contained and controlled by BPP cadres.

But starting in the 70s, the FBI's COINTELPRO Program (a portmanteau derived from *CO*unter *INTEL*ligence *PRO*gram) actively worked to suppress the efforts of the BPP through the numerous arrests, infiltration, incarceration, and exile of BPP members. This had a significant impact on the BPP and its core mission, causing fractures and dissent within its once-powerful and organized structure. As the BPP struggled to fight off the COINTELPRO operatives, this distraction allowed a new gangster ethos to emerge on the street that ultimately derailed the movement and changed an entire culture.

Every meeting, every court date, and every celebration nurtured Tupac's warrior spirit and laid the foundation of the responsibilities he faced to bring the people closer to liberation and peace. Seeing up close the Lincoln Hospital Detox program and its immediate impact on addicts taught him respect for humanity and the power of unifying people from all walks of life. He absorbed these bold lessons of empowerment, resolute with the knowledge that true liberation comes from solving our own oppression with love, intelligence, and courage. He was a witness that all things are achievable with unity and courage. He testified to these teachings every day of his life.

He learned these truths because he was exposed to the greatness of ordinary people working together tirelessly and sacrificing everything to build a better world. We had strong connections to our unions, as labor movements historically represented the workers' demands for decent wages in New York City. We worked diligently in the prisoner rights movements, filing federal lawsuits exposing human rights' violations of prisoners and its impact on families. We were on the front lines fighting against the drugs which devastated our communities. He observed firsthand that people can be mobilized as we marched against the Board of Education or with the hospital workers' unions. Tupac learned the power of one's voice from these movements and he learned the art of defiance, its rhythm, and its power.

Through these experiences, he also discovered that social justice must have a component of economic advancement and knowing this, he sought that economic independence through his art.

No matter the place or situation, Tupac was a natural leader. He brought out the best in everyone because he always gave his best efforts in everything he did and he expected the same from all that were around him.

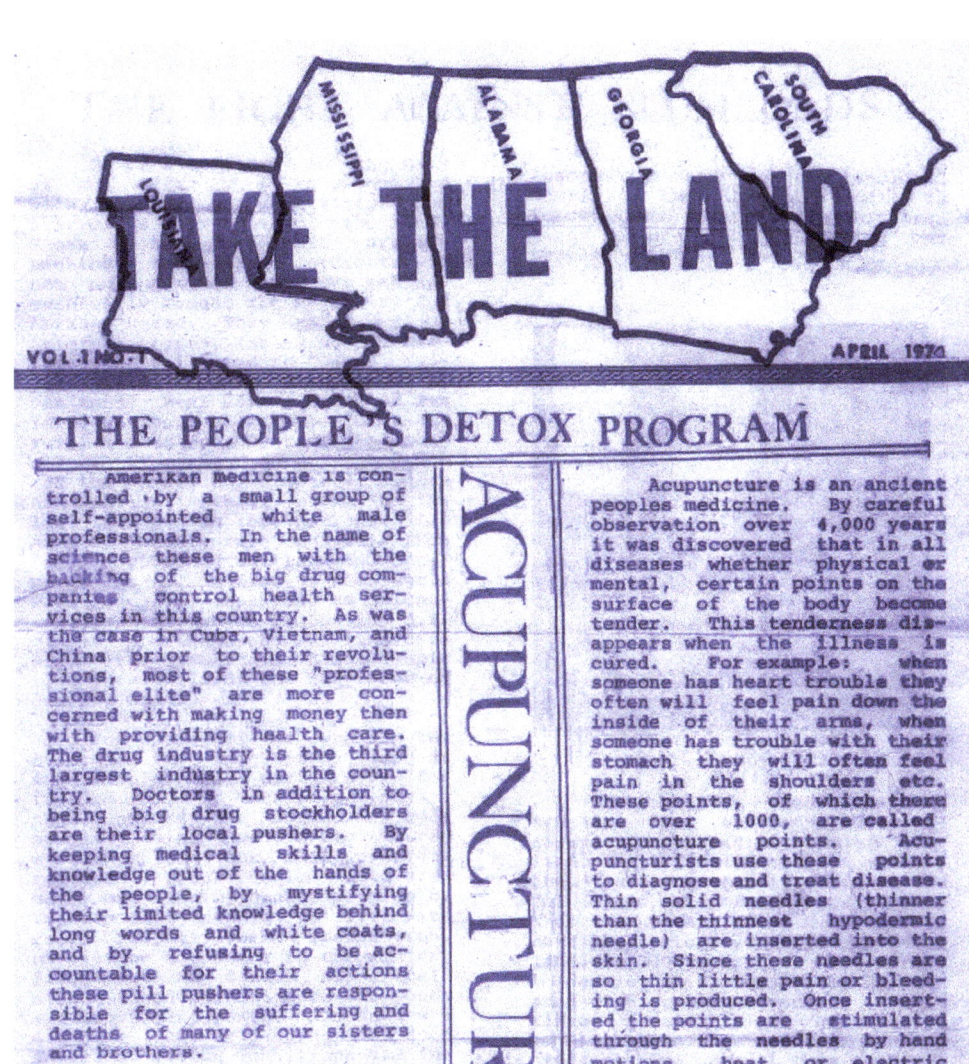

(above) Page from one of our mimeographed publications–printed by Tupac— sharing information about the acupuncture program.

WEST SIDE -*The Call*

In 1977, Afeni, Mutulu, and I founded the National Task Force for COINTELPRO Litigation and Research (NTFCLR). Using the Freedom of Information Act, we researched the role the FBI played in the infiltration, surveillance, and eventual demise of the BPP. People who had been targeted requested copies of FBI files to determine what records were kept on Panthers and we connected the dots of all this information. Starting in the 60s, many activists (not only from the BPP but many other organizations, too) were incarcerated, went underground or into exile, and also died in the aftermath.

Geronimo Pratt was one of our clients with NTFCLR. The NTFCLR's board of directors included some of the most prominent activists of the time: Lennox Hinds, Dr. Nathan Hare, Noam Chomsky, and Flo Kennedy. We were dedicated to helping organizations and individuals targeted by the COINTELPRO secure their government files. Many activists, and especially the leadership of the BPP such as Geronimo, were falsely charged with crimes as a direct result of their work with the Panther Party resulting in their incarceration, or having to go underground to avoid incarceration, or death.

In 1979 while our Legal Services offices were on strike, we packed up Yaki, Sekyiwa, and Tupac, and traveled to San Francisco to work on Geronimo's lawsuit against the US Government. He was incarcerated at San Quentin. The fact that there was a targeting of activists was established after the Senate Church Committee in 1975 exposed the illegal intelligence activities of the FBI's COINTELPRO, which confirmed what we had been saying all along—that the destruction of the Black Panther Party and the incarceration and death of hundreds of Black Panthers was the result of a carefully orchestrated program developed by J. Edgar Hoover and perpetrated against the progressive forces of the Black Liberation Movement.

We were able to prove through the Freedom of Information Act (known as FOIA) and the release of Geronimo Pratt's files that he had been framed by the United States Government and that the main witness against him was a government informant. We worked tirelessly on many cases to expose the conspiracy by FBI to "discredit" and "neutralize" all leadership of the Black Panther Party. G's case was one of the first to accumulate proof positive through release of FOIA documents that a conspiracy did indeed exist against him.

The nature of the relationship shared by Yafeu and Tupac was always one of protection and love. No matter what, Tupac was always sharing what he had with Yaki–here it's a rock, symbolic of their eternal brotherhood.

Tupac and Yaki, San Francisco, ca '79.

    We stayed in the Mission District thanks to the benevolent activists also working on G's case. I was eager to work on this case and it was my first time in the infamous San Quentin visiting room.

    I remember G telling us how he tried in vain to explain to Johnny Cochran, who represented him at the criminal trial, that he was set up by powers outside of the police forces. He told Johnny there was a national conspiracy to detain and destroy him because of his Army training and these orders were coming from government agencies. Johnny was unaccustomed to representing Panthers as he was just starting out as a criminal defense lawyer. He was dismissive of G's claims and thought he was being overly paranoid. Johnny Cochran later conceded his mistake in underestimating the scope of the conspiracy against black revolutionaries like Geronimo.

G was the person who gave me my last name of Fula, stating my attributes were that of the culturally diverse Fula/Fulani tribes of western Africa. Years later, during tracing of my African ancestry, I learned through mitochondrial DNA testing on my mother's side my ancestors were traced to the Tikar people from western Africa, Cameroon. So in his infinite wisdom, Geronimo was right on point as the Fula tribes hailed from western Africa.

Tupac was surrounded at a very early age with men and women who were the defenders of the culture, defenders of the people. Alliances were made with people from all walks of life, races and genders. Coalitions and close ties were forged during this time to defend Panthers and their supporters who had been targeted and incarcerated for their politics.

Geronimo was Tupac's godfather. He was one of the links in the chain of resistance to tyranny that taught Tupac the meaning of honorable resistance. Honor is attained by choosing what is best for all people and not what is best for the individual. Geronimo, Sekou, and Mutulu all made enormous sacrifices. Tupac gave homage in his songs to their lives and the pain endured by their families, including on his final album with the song "Hold Ya Head":

> **MY HOMEBOYS IN CLINTON AND RIKERS ISLAND**
> **ALL THE PENITENTIARIES**
> **MUMIA, MUTULU, GERONIMO, SEKOU!**
> **ALL THE POLITICAL PRISONERS**
> **SAN QUENTIN (WHO CAN SAVE YOU?)... ALL THE JAILHOUSES**
> **I'M WITH YOU**

These were Tupac's Redemption Songs, his songs of freedom, in tune with ancestors such as the late great Bob Marley. He studied his predecessors who used their voices to condemn war and destruction of the land. Poverty horrified Tupac; he had seen it up close and personal. He decided as a youngster to use his voice to expose the sufferings of people. "These songs of freedom, is all I ever have...redemption songs..."

Lewis Myers, Jr., a prominent Chicago movement attorney, worked with the Task Force attorneys representing G in court. We reviewed thousands of pages of FBI files. But even though there were FOIA requests, the papers to prove G's innocence took years to compile due to heavy redactions.

In 1997, G's conviction was overturned after 27 years on the grounds that the government informant lied. Geronimo passed away in June 2011 in Tanzania, finally free after sacrificing so many years in service towards a better world.

During our visit to San Francisco to work on Geronimo's case, we drove down to visit my friends Maria and John Carlos. We brought G's little baby Shona with us but left Tupac, Sekyiwa, and Yaki in San Francisco for the weekend. John was one of our heroes growing up. He and Tommy Davis were the athletes that raised their fists in protest to the conditions and treatment of blacks in the US during the 1968 Olympics ceremony in Mexico. This single act of courage embarrassed the United States in front of the world and revealed America's best kept secret: that racism was alive and well in the US.

John became an instant hero in the black liberation movement but that came at enormous sacrifice. Upon returning to the US, he was vilified by the press and he lost the prospects of lucrative sports endorsements. This took a lot of courage. Salute to John Carlos, Maria Butler, their children and grandchildren, and their entire family for their sacrifices in the name of liberation and justice that greatly influenced both Tupac and Yaki.

John Carlos and his daughter Shana, ca '79.

(left) American sprinters Tommie Smith and John Carlos, along with Australian Peter Norman, during the award ceremony of the 200 m race at the Mexican Olympic games. During the awards ceremony, Smith (center) and Carlos protested against racial discrimination: they went barefoot on the podium and listened to their anthem bowing their heads and raising a fist with a black glove. Mexico City, '68. Photo by Angelo Cozzi.

(below) John Carlos on left, Afeni holding Geronimo's baby Shona, ca '79.

(opposite top) Afeni, Lewis Myers, Jr., and colleague attending hearings in San Francisco for Geronimo.

(opposite bottom) Geronimo in court challenging his conviction with Lewis Myers Jr. In those days you could bring a camera in court. I'm so glad I had mine!

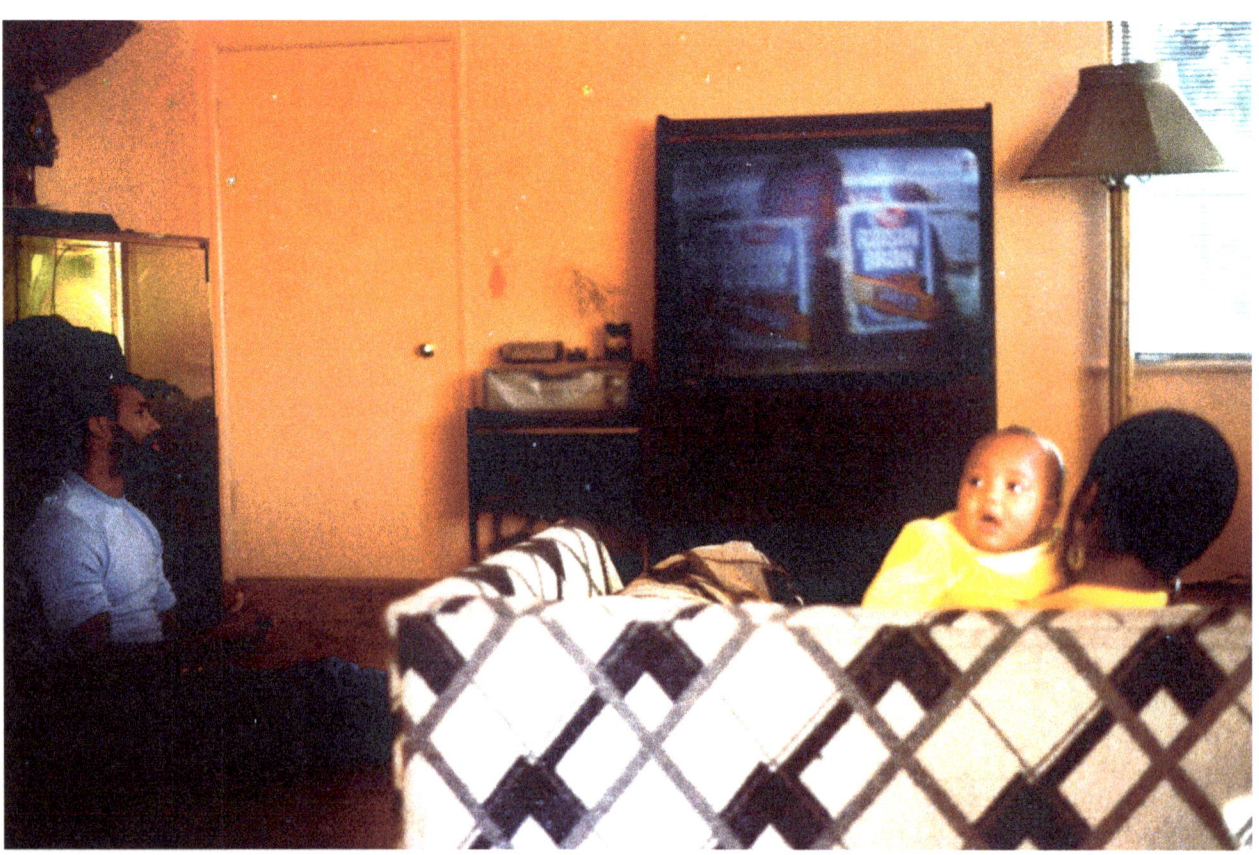

Tupac, Yaki, and Sekyiwa during Geronimo's legal appeals, Mission District, San Francisco, ca '79.

Metropolitan Correctional Center –
Belly of the Beast~ No Snitching

In October 1981 during an armored car robbery, several guards were killed and a number of members of the Weather Underground and Black Liberation Army were implicated. Several people arrested at the scene of the robbery had been underground and were wanted by the FBI for many years. They were conscientious anti-war activists who were forced underground during the 60s. It was the first time the so-called Weather Underground fugitives were implicated with members of the Black Liberation Army and Panthers at the scene of a robbery. It was as if a nuclear bomb had been dropped on all activists, organizers, sympathizers, and advocates for justice in New York. The ensuing raids, investigations, arrests, and subpoenas wreaked havoc on the activist community in New York at the time. Many refused to cooperate with what was termed a witch hunt using the bank robbery as pretext to disrupt legitimate work being done by decent folks.

The federal grand jury had unlimited subpoena power and operated in total secrecy. It has always been used as a weapon to attack liberation struggles and anti-imperialist movements in this country. The goal was to obtain information about political organizers and to criminalize their legitimate right to dissent. The aftermath was devastating. Eight were charged with bank robbery, under the RICO Act (Racketeer Influenced and Corrupt Organizations Act), which included the escape of Assata Shakur from prison in 1978. Six were eventually convicted, four people died, and several families were destroyed with children now growing up without mothers and fathers.

When this all started, I was a paralegal at Bronx Legal Services. I was also secretary for NTFCLR. Our job was to expose the clandestine operation of COINTELPRO by the FBI and the role it played in targeting people for their affiliations with organizations and neutralizing activists who fled the country, went underground, or went to jail.

Sekou was arrested in my car after a high-speed chase in Queens. The shootout resulted in one brother, Mtayari Sundiata, being killed by police and Sekou's arrest and torture. The federal grand jury was convened to investigate the Brinks bank robbery with broad subpoena powers and they subpoenaed me.

Collaboration was not an option. When you collaborate, you work together to create something both benefit from. There was no collaboration with the government, only a deep quest to disrupt, discredit, and neutralize the movement.

We knew I was going to jail because I refused to testify and I refused to collaborate even though I'd been subpoenaed. Unlike the Mueller grand jury subpoenas of today, there was no negotiation with my attorney to determine if I would appear. There were no options.

I did not stop at Go.

There were no free rolls of the dice.

I went straight to jail.

I was not allowed to have an attorney present during these secret proceedings. But I was allowed to read my statement. It was an explanation of why I refused to testify, who I was, and why the subpoena violated my constitutional rights. The state and the federal governments wanted blood, hair samples, and snitches. None of which I had any desire to give.

After much wrangling, many court proceedings, and attempts by my dear friend and lawyer Lewis Myers, Jr. to delay the inevitable, I went to jail around November 1981. MCC did not intimidate me. I had been going in and out of MCC visiting Dhoruba Moore and other clients. NTFCLR represented many ex-Panthers still incarcerated as a result of illegal FBI activities. We did the research, worked with the lawyers, and under FOIA, we obtained FBI memorandums which proved our clients were indeed set up and targeted for their Constitutionally-protected political activities.

But this time was different. I was the inmate and not a visitor. The guards recognized me. They were mostly African American. They treated me with respect. I will never forget someone had posted a sign over the entrance way to the women's floor—5 South. "Abandon All Hope Ye Who Enters These Doors." That brought a little chuckle as I walked through them. After spending all night in the bullpen being processed, I was glad to finally be on the floor. I was not expecting to be thrown immediately into the solitary confinement for administrative segregation. I was not charged with a crime, only civil contempt. MCC was in complete violation of my rights by labeling me a security risk so they could place me in the notorious hole. However, there was Kathy Boudin on one side, Judy Clarke on the other.

Visits from my attorney and family were denied. Additionally, it was against institutional rules to throw me in the hole as I was not charged with any crime but that didn't stop them from doing that. I was merely found in contempt of civil court. Their intent was to break me. I did my crying in the pillow so the jailers did not hear my anguish. After several days, I went on a hunger strike. It was important to never show any weakness. I remember reading later other courageous women recollect their days of imprisonment—Ericka Huggins, Assata Shakur, Angela Davis—and the discipline it took to never, ever let them see you cry.

It was soon clear to the feds that "I Am Not Your Negro."

I did what I had to do. I went on a hunger strike.

The announcement on the NY radio stations was widespread. "Yaasmyn Fula, a mother and paralegal at Bronx Legal Services, has gone on a hunger strike protesting jail conditions after being arrested and found in civil contempt by a federal grand jury investigating the Brinks armored car robbery." The guards were instructed to keep a log every day I refused food. I guess this was to determine at what point they would intervene and decide whether to force feed. At first, they were writing in the log. It was so easy to refuse that food because it was horrible. But as the days went on, I guess I was starting to look really gaunt and they would encourage me to eat the fruit. I said I would if they would not report that in their log. The MCC higher-ups did not want a situation where someone not even charged with a crime is on hunger strike protesting her treatment and then dies. So I needed them to think I was not eating anything to force them to release me to general population.

While in the hole, I was let out of my cell for one hour daily to shower and make phone calls. During my walks to and from the shower to the phone, the women showed solidarity. "Anything you need? We got you!" They would come to my cell window with information about the case and encouragement, always sneaking me something to eat. It was always the sisterhood of women that sustained me. The shared rage of confinement always transforming creatively by the women to help each other survive.

In the prison world, the correctional officers (aka COs) were just as much inmates as the inmates. Someone charged with not cooperating with the grand jury, ready to come to jail, and now on hunger strike, garnered the respect of COs. I was soon released from the hole and put out into general population.

In 1981, Rudy Giuliani was the New York State Attorney General in charge of prosecutions for all major federal indictments. While RICO was more commonly known for its use against mafia families, this was the first time RICO was used against members of the Black liberation struggle and Anti-imperialist movements. The Witness Protection Program was filled up with former mafia members now testifying against their bosses. During the Brinks robbery trial, there were also those who entered the Witness Protection Program and testified against their comrades.

COLLABORATION WAS NOT AN OPTION. WHEN YOU COLLABORATE, YOU WORK TOGETHER TO CREATE SOMETHING BOTH BENEFIT FROM. THERE WAS NO COLLABORATION WITH THE GOVERNMENT, ONLY A DEEP QUEST TO DISRUPT, DISCREDIT, AND NEUTRALIZE THE MOVEMENT.

The Gambino crew always expressed maximum respect for our "non-collaboration, non-snitching" position. They were always sending presents to the "broads on 5S" out of respect. When escorted to our visits with attorneys, in the prison hallways Gotti's crew and others would always acknowledge us… "Anything you's need from the kitchen, let us know." You better believe I did.

The notorious Nicky "Mr. Untouchable" Barnes controlled a vast heroin empire in Harlem. He testified against members of his organization, including his wife Thelma Grant. The flamboyant lifestyle of cars, clothing and jewelry comes at a tremendous cost of loss of life, betrayal, and a community addicted to drugs. We were all just prison numbers. People from so many different backgrounds now converged into a manned fortress trying to survive.

Women who didn't know me but understood my stance gave support and comfort. Correction officers, now my jailers, showed respect balancing that fine blue line. Mafia bosses, drug lords, and foot soldiers were always sending food to acknowledge our stance of non-collaboration. Then there was the dear Kosher cook, who fed us all. The Chef kept us alive with his special recipes and hidden gifts.

He was a rabbi of sorts, always with a quote from the Torah, but quick to knock out intruders who crossed the line. There was always that fine line in jail you do not cross. I learned so much about the human spirit while a prisoner at MCC. I also learned how to make moonshine. It made me deathly ill. A simple step in the distillation process was ignored. Too many heads, not enough hearts. Moonshine must have proper temperature controls and time spent to distillate it properly. The "heads" must be removed, not consumed. The middle part, the "hearts", is the best part. But it was Christmas and the women were impatient to have a lil' drink to dull the holiday blues.

Too many heads, not enough hearts will always lead to disaster.

I was certainly in familiar territory, only this time instead of 100 Centre Street or the Women's House of Detention, the protests were outside the Federal Courts in lower Manhattan and the Metropolitan Correctional Facility. Unlike the House of D where women could call out from the barred windows to family or protesters in the streets below, there would be none of that at MCC. The Women's House of Detention on Greenwich Avenue was demolished in 1974. It was replaced with a garden, no doubt watered by the sweat and tears of its former inhabitants. *How in the world did Afeni with baby Tupac in her belly survive the notorious and deplorable rat-infested conditions?* The cries for justice and freedom on the steps of these institutions were all too familiar but now, some ten years later, I was on the other side of the wall peering out from behind prison windows that did not open.

So many great people came together during this time of intense state and federal attempt to criminalize political dissent. The Grand Jury Project, the Center for Constitutional Rights, National Organization of Legal Services Workers, and countless others gave me sustenance during these very difficult days.

The anguish for me was being separated from my son, Yafeu. The media hype and propaganda around the Brinks case created an atmosphere of division and fear. I was told my son could come to see me but I could not touch him and he could not touch me. He might have a weapon. He was only four years old at the time. It was just another attempt to break me down. I rejected their terms So I didn't see my son during my incarceration. I did however get a few visits from my beloved Tupac. He updated me and gave me such strength during those times in the visiting room. He understood we couldn't touch. He was only ten years old but in his boyish enthusiasm always tried to give reassurances Yaki was fine by telling me all the funny stuff he was doing.

Yaki performed on the song "As the World Turns" with Tupac and the Outlawz on the album *Still I Rize*. His verse had a very special meaning to both Tupac and Yaki. It was a tribute to their solidarity and bond of brotherhood shared at tender ages of four and ten, during those dark days.

> **October 9th 1977 first day out my baby carriage**
> **Married my Mac-11 hit the block playin'**
> **Only 5 years up in this bitch**
> **Papa runnin' from the feds**
> **Puttin' peanut butter on the walls**
> **to hide his prints...**

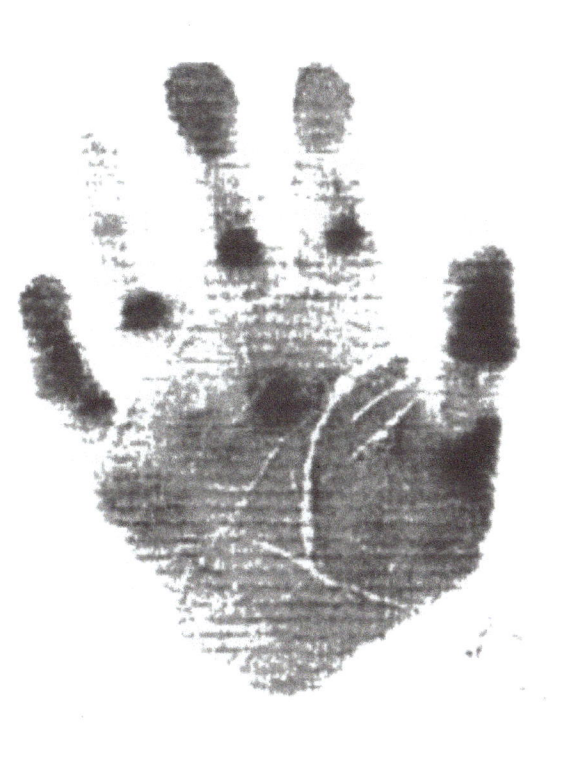
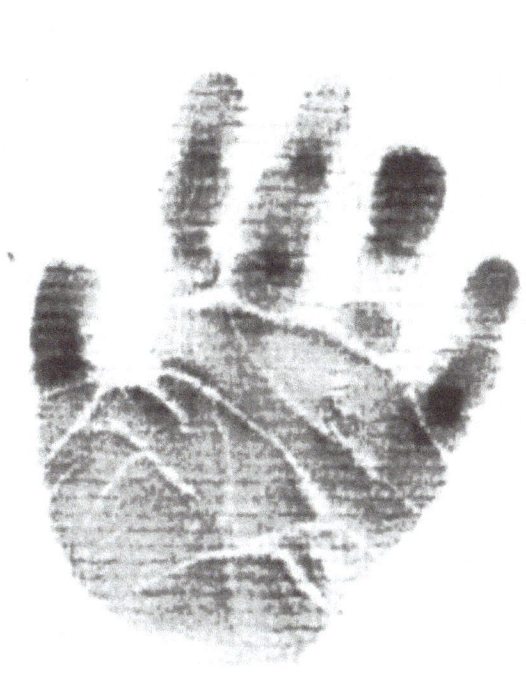

So many great people and organizations supported me during my 18-month incarceration: labor movements, anti-war movements, prisoners rights organizations, criminal justice law firms. I thought about Harriet Tubman navigating the Underground Railroad in search of a better life, being chased but never giving up.

Bilal Sunni-Ali – known to all of us as "Spirit" – with his daughter on his shoulders. Bilal was the saxophone player with Gil Scott Heron and the Midnight Band. He was married to Fulani Sunni-Ali (shown in the Quash article to the right). Photo taken outside MCC, ca '82.

QUASH
newsletter of the GRAND JURY PROJECT, INC.

Volume 7, Number 1   January/February 1982

Government Starts Witchhunt
Four Subpoenaed to New York RICO Grand Jury

In November, four women were subpoenaed to appear before a federal grand jury in New York City that is allegedly looking into the attempted robbery in October of a Brinks truck in Nanuet, New York. Three of the women, Eve Rosahn, Fulani Sunni-Ali and Yaasmyn Fula refused to cooperate with the grand jury and were cited for contempt and jailed. Sunni-Ali and Rosahn, both released from jail in December, along with the fourth woman, Jerry Gaines, are still fighting subpoenas.

The grand jury, convened in the Southern District of New York (Manhattan) shortly after the robbery attempt, is allegedly investigating "conspiracy" charges under the Racketeer Influenced and Corrupt Organization Act. Passed in 1970, along with the infamous Organized Crime Control Act RICO, as the act is commonly known, provides the government with enormous latitude. Those subpoenaed to the grand jury, their attorneys and others are charging that RICO, which was supposedly intended for "organized crime," is being improperly used in this investigation.

Immediately after the robbery attempt on October 20, during which one guard and two police officers were killed, four people were arrested and accused of allegedly having participated in it: Kathy Boudin and David Gilbert who originally gave alias and who have in the past been associated the the Weather Underground; Judy Clark, a member of the above-ground May 19th Communist Organization; and Samuel Smith, a Black man not identified with any group.

Raids, False Arrests, Murder

As soon as the identities of those accused of being involved in the robbery became known, the FBI and the police announced that they were launching a "broadside investigation into the incident."

"We are looking at this as a major racketeering investigation," Kenneth Walton, director of the Federal-New York City Terrorism Task Force stated in an interview with reporters. The Task Force, Walton continued, would "look at possible links between these groups and possibly some foreign organizations." Although no links had yet been found, Walton went on to say that the groups shared some common purposes,

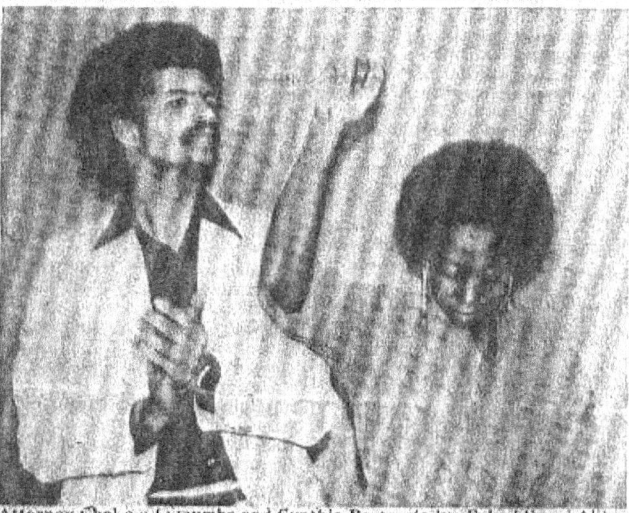

Attorney Chokwe Lumumba and Cynthia Boston (a/k/a Fulani Sunni-Ali)

including, the desire to "an end of the U.S. government as we know it" and "the creation of a socialist state."

Walton's announcement and several events in the days folowing the robbery fueled charges that the government was using the incident to conduct a campaign of harassment against left and progressive groups, particularly those associated with the Black liberation movement. It was charged that "terrorist," a label much used by the FBI and the media, was being used as a code-word for "communist," "subversive," and in particular "Black."

On October 23, police officers in Queens chased a car that the said bore a license plate that had been linked to the robbery. When the chase was over, one of the car's two Black occupants, Mtayari Sundiata, laid dead on the ground, and the other, Sekou Odinga, was in handcuffs. The police officers who claimed that Sundiata was killed in a "gun battle" and were reportedly heard to say jubilantly over the radio "we win one," left Sundiata's body lying on the ground to be photographed by news reporters. These pictures were later plastered on the covers or inside several commerical newspapers. Odinga's transfer to King's County Hospital fifteen hours after his arrest further raised questions about the conduct of the police. Odinga and his attorneys charged that in the four and a half hours after his arrival at the 112th Precinct in Queens, Odinga was taken into three different rooms where several officers hit him on the head, put his head in a toilet, burned his wrists with cigars and threatened to shoot him.

"He (a police officer) put a gun to my head and asked me where was somebody I didn't know," Odinga told a reporter form the *New York Times* in an interview conducted in the prison ward at King's County on October 28. "I said I didn't know, and he pulled the trigger and it went 'click.' He asked me four more questions and clicked the gun four more times."

Eleven weeks later, Odinga is still at King's County, where, it is being charged, he is being denied proper medical treatment. Samuel Smith, who was beaten by the police after his arrest on the 20th, was also recently transferred to a hospital.

Also on the 23rd, the FBI raided the home of Eleanor Stein Raskin and Jeffrey Jones, two members of the Weather Underground, whose attorney was in the process of negotiating their surrender on old un-related charges, and arrested them. Though the government refused to say what led them to arrest Jones and Raskin and failed to produce any evidence linking them to Nanuet, they were held on $150,000 and $100,000 bail respectively. Newspapers also printed reports linking them to the robbery.

Neither Jones or Raskin received prison sentences on the old charges, and neither were indicted by the Rockland County state grand jury that handed down indictments against Boudin, Clark, Gilbert, Brown, Odinga, Rosahn, Marilyn Buck and Anthony LaBorde. Laborde was arrested in Philadelphia by local police on January 7 and brought back to New York with almost fifty stitches in his head, and placed on $10 million bail. Buck is still being sought.

On October 27, the government was at it again, this time in New York and Mississippi. In one of two New York incidents on the 27, FBI agents and local police raided two apartments before locating Eve Rosahn at a friend's apartment. Rosahn, an anti-imperialist activist already facing charges as a result of her participation in a Kennedy airport demonstration against the South African Rugby team, the government claimed, had lent her car and rented another for use by the alleged robbers.

Meanwhile, in Garden City, Long Island, a SWAT team composed of thirty local and county police officers, armed with an "anonymous" tip that Assata Shakur was in a van were arriving at a home where four Black cleaning workers were employed. The team, all wearing flak vests and carrying shot-

(continued on page 11)

News Flash

As we were going to press, Yaasmyn Fula, was released on bail pending the resolution of her appeal of her contempt citation. Fula's release came less than a week after federal Judge Whitman Knapp denied her application for bail and termed her appeal "frivolous." The Second Circuit Court of Appeals, which reserved decision in the case, obviously felt different. If her appeal is denied, however, Fula, could he rejailed. She also faces a second subpoena for testimony.

In other developments, charges linking Eve Rosahn to the robbery attempt in Nanuet were dropped after her legal defense team produced evidence proving that she could not have been the person who rented the van used in the robbery attempt. On January 20, Donald Weems, a former member of the Black Panther Party, was arrested and accused of allegedly having taken part in the robbery.

Chokwe Lumumba and Fulani Sunni-Ali pictured above in Quash article.

STATEMENT OF YAASMYN D. FULA TO BE READ TO THE GRAND JURY ON DECEMBER 2, 1981

Members of the Grand Jury:

I appear before you today not in repudiation of orderliness and due process but rather in defense of these very ethics to which I have been bound and have committed my life to. You are the people of the same communities in which I live, in which I raise my adoring 4-year-old son, and whom I have represented as a paralegal for Bronx Legal Services. As a paralegal at Bronx Legal Services for nine years, I have been sworn to abide by the Canon Code of Ethics in my representations of your neighbors, your sons, daughters, and acquaintances in legal civil proceedings throughout New. York City. No body politic or lawful proceeding should expect me to now violate these codes of conduct.

For these reasons, it is imperative to me that you be able to balance your legal and ethical duties. Towards that end, you must have a factual understanding for why I have refused compliance with your requests. For I, too, am fulfilling my destiny to convene on the plight of our social order. My work however, has already been vindicated by a higher order, so I am here before you not in pursuit of your endorsement. Rather it is the future of our society and laws of mankind that is at stake, and preoccupies my statement today.

I believe I have been subpoenaed before this Grand Jury as a direct result of my association with the National Task Force for COINTELPRO Litigation and Research. This organization of lawyers, activists, and legal researchers was convened after revelations by the Select Committee of the United States Senate (Church Committee) that the FBI and other governmental agencies spied on, illegally surveilled, illegally tapped and monitored phone conversations, for purposes of disrupting legitimate and constitutionally protected dissent against unjust laws of society. This program, known as COINTELPRO, was meant to gather intelligence on individuals who were members of or known associates of organizations engaged in constitutional redress through a host of criminal and illegal means.

As a result of my work with this human rights organization that sought vindication of the innocent victims of the FBI's ruthless campaign through our litigation and education efforts, I have now become a victim of the very same violations. My phone conversations have been illegally monitored, and I have been threatened with imprisonment unless I reveal the content of conversations I have had with clients of the NTFCLR, in clear violation of the attorney-client privilege I am sworn to uphold.

I ask only that during the course of your investigation you seek out answers to my assertions and not accept mere dismissal of them as frivolous. It is even less imperative that I be spared the unjustness of incarceration than it is that we spare society further abuse against the Constitution we hold dear. Take your time, ladies and gentlemen, as you inquire with open minds. If my going to jail means equity and fair-minded application of the laws shall prevail, then I await the inglorious place to which fate has placed me.

During Afeni's incarceration, she had to petition the federal court to get permission for more nutritious meals and milk during the Panther 21 trial. She was pregnant with Tupac and we held vigil outside the Women's House of Detention in lower Manhattan. We marched and we made plenty of noise as her petition went before the Chief Judge of the United States District Court Constance B. Motley. Judge Motley not only served with Thurgood Marshall's legal team at the NAACP Legal Defense and Educational Fund in 1945 but was also chief counsel for James Meredith in his legal battle to attend the University of Mississippi, arguing the case before the US Supreme Court. She was on the front lines of the civil rights movement in its early beginnings. We felt vindicated when Afeni's case went before her as she was the first black woman appointed to the federal bench, despite lots of opposition. We always felt we had an ally in Judge Motley's courtroom. We fought against the same indignities of racism, sexism, poverty, and ignorance.

In 1983 during my 18-month long incarceration for refusing to cooperate with the federal grand jury, myself and my seven comrades (also civil contemnors) wrote Judge Motley a letter seeking release from prison on the grounds that it was punitive and unconstitutional.

Just like Afeni, I found myself appearing before the same Judge Motley, representing myself in court to challenge the unconstitutionality of the laws. I could hear the women and supporters marching outside MCC, demanding our freedom. It was déjà vu as history repeated itself. During those long lonely days as my soul lamented freedom, the words of Teena Marie's "Déjà Vu" ran through my mind…

> **I'm young and I'm old**
> **I'm rich and I'm poor**
> **I feel like I've been on this earth many times before**
> **Once I was a white gazelle**
> **On a horseback riding free**
> **Searching in the darkness**
> **For a piece of me……**
> **I can feel this for sure**
> **I been here before…..**

On March 1, 1983, Judge Motley granted my motion to proceed in forma pauperis (indigent). But before my petition was heard, I was released because after 18 months, the federal government was bound by law to either release me or convene another grand jury to re-subpoena. The prosecutors were forced to concede we were not going to cooperate and I was released in June 1983, after the convictions in the Brinks bank robbery trial.

Many friendships were forged during this time with people from all walks of life at MCC. Many friendships were also destroyed, never again to be restored. Such are the spoils of war.

Karate films were all over the theaters back then. After all, it was the 80s!! I took the children to all the Bruce Lee movies on 42nd Street. They were obsessive little soldiers running around throwing karate chops, jumping through the air, and flying off couches and beds with no fear. It seems like all they ever did was jump through the air showing off their latest karate techniques.

Standing on the steps of MCC showing off their best karate moves was their youthful way of standing up to these ominous concrete walls. This was very important to them and even Sekyiwa had her own moves.

Metropolitan Correction Center, the only federal jail in lower Manhattan, was the holding center for people not yet convicted but charged with federal crimes, e.g., narcotics, organized crime, forgery, and robbery. I would be going back to MCC soon but cooperating with the FBI's attack on the Black movement was not an option. The children understood this position and were very supportive.

I wanted Yaki to see where I would be staying. I even pointed to the windows on 5S. Since he couldn't visit me due to the prison security rules, I told him we would arrange a day when he would be outside and I would wave to him.

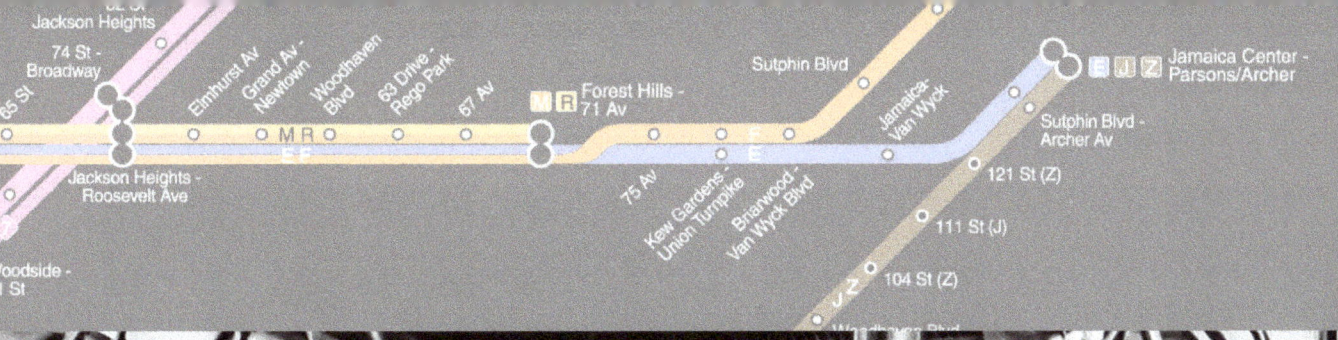

Around December 1981, I was out on bail from the grand jury subpoena on a technicality. Afeni and I gathered up the children for an adventure in NYC. We made a day of it and went to Chinatown for lunch. It was fun for them and took the stress off of the reality that my bail was a temporary glitch.

Lo and behold, we had the whole train to ourselves. Tupac, Sekyiwa, and Yaki were thrilled! In New York when you are the only one on the train you do one of two things, get off at the next stop or, as it was with the children— PERFORM!!! That empty subway car became a jungle gym as the children went swinging from strap to strap, thrilled at the freedom of not being told to sit down. When I pulled out the camera, they knew it was on!!

(top left) Katari, Tupac, and Yaki eating Chinese food.

(top right) Tupac, Yaki, and Sekyiwa.

(bottom from left)

Yaki riding his bike in East Orange, NJ.

Cheryl Davila and Yaki (notice Sharonda clowning in the back!), Metropolitan Museum of Natural History, NYC, one of our favorite places to visit.

Yaasmyn, Sharonda Davila, and Yaki.

Yaki and Sharonda.

SEKOU ODINGA - YAKI'S FATHER

Look for Me in the Whirlwind or the Storm...

Yaki's father, Sekou Odinga, was forced underground in 1969 during the Black Panther Party New York 21 trial. The leadership of the Black Panther Party was the target of raids by state and local police in New York and across the country. The FBI launched a "concerted program" to divide the Black Panther Party and its East Coast/West Coast leadership by targeting its members and their sympathizers. Sekou was caught in October 1981 when he was arrested in the aftermath of the Brink's armored car robbery. During his capture, Sekou was tortured and charged with participating in the liberation of Assata Shakur and association with the Black Liberation Army.

In 1983, Sekou was sentenced to forty years to life under the RICO Act. During the trial in his opening statement, Sekou claimed he was a fighter for the freedom of New Afrikans, that he was a descendant of Afrikan slaves, and as such, denied equal citizenship in America. Sekou proclaimed to the jury his resistance has led to his capture and, according to the Geneva Convention and International Law, must be treated as a prisoner of war and not a criminal. It was a bold and unprecedented position that was both courageous and hugely sacrificial for his family. I knew from the day he stood up to read this profound declaration in court that his son, Yafeu, would grow up without his father.

Like all boys, Yaki needed his father to survive America. Growing up without the guidance and protection of a father was more than either Tupac or Yafeu could endure. Attempts by fatherly surrogates to exercise some menial parental norms were quickly rejected by the boys, as it was all too late with too little. At a very early age, Tupac threw a safety net around Yafeu because he knew that standing strong for freedom came with a price—especially for the men.

We celebrated Sekou's birthday every year on June 17 and Tupac's birthday every year on June 16. It was how we kept the memories alive for the children of their fathers' sacrifices, their absence always painfully present in the eyes of the boys.

(right) Judith Clark (with fist raised), Sekou Odinga, David Gilbert and co-defendants being led from courtroom during the Brinks armored car robbery trial, 1983. Illustration courtesy of Marilyn Church.

The murder of our son, Yafeu, was particularly hard for Sekou as he was incarcerated in 1996 when it happened. Yaki was only four years old when in 1981 Sekou was captured and I refused to testify before the federal grand jury and went straight to jail. The blow was especially hard for Yafeu as he was now bounced from one household to another. But through these trying times, Tupac, once again, put his loving arms around his little brother.

Paroled in 2014 on a technicality after serving 33 years in prison, Sekou remains a committed advocate for the human rights of Afrikan Americans. Tupac gave homage on his final album to them in the song "White Man'z World":

> **Use your brain, use your brain**
> **It ain't them that's killin' us; it's US that's killin' us**
> **It ain't them that's knockin' us off; it's US that's knockin' us off**
> **I'm telling you better watch it or be a victim**
> **Be a victim in this white man's world**
> **Born black in this white man's world, no doubt**
> **And it's dedicated to my motherfuckin' teachers**
> **Mutulu Shakur, Geronimo Pratt, Mumia Abu Jamal, Sekou Odinga,**
> **And all the real OGs, we out!**

We Demand Prisoner of War Status

Comrade Odinga's Opening Statement:

My name is Sekou Abdullah Odinga. I am a Muslim and a freedom fighter, a New Afrikan Freedom Fighter.

The name Abdullah means servant of God in Arabic. I chose that name because i try to be a servant of God. I try to do the will of God. I believe it is God's will to fight oppression and to enjoin what is right. That is why i am here today because i have been fighting oppression and trying to enjoin what i think is right all my adult life.

I am a political being. I have been a part of the Black Liberation movement, the movement to free Black people from the oppression and the injustices that they have suffered since first being brought here as Afrikan slaves. I am a descendent of those Afrikan slaves. That's why the rest of my name, Sekou Odinga, is an Afrikan name. I gave up the name Nathaniel Burns, which indeed i was born with, because the name Burns, was passed down from my ancetors' slavemaster and i do not wish to be a slave any more. So becoming grown and thinking for myself i changed my name.

As you probably know, Afrikan people in America, unlike most people, were first brought here to be slaves. That was the only reason they came. Other ethnic groups came here to reap the benefits of a free America. Afrikans didn't come for that reason. They were brought here to create those benefits for the colonialists, the white people that were here.

From the first time that my people made contact with the agents of the colonialists, they fought. They didn't come here willingly. They fought against that slavery & they continued to fight it throughout their time here. There were many slave rebellions & many slaves escapes, many attempts of rebellion and attempts of escapes. So Afrikan people here didn't really accept those conditions that they were in. It was forced on them.

At the time the people in this country were colonialized, there were 13 British colonies. They didn't want to be colonies because when you are colonialized everything that you produce, all the wealth that your produce goes to the colonializer or the mother country. And that was happening here at the same time that they were enslaving us, they were being colonialized by Great Britian. So they decided that they would step forward as men and women and take their place in the world as a free nation and so declared themselves so and started to fight for their freedom. Because, like always, those who are controlling, and reaping large benefits don't want to give it up.

So they had what they call an American revolution.

Well, today there is another revolution going on. I call it the New Afrikan Revolution. I am a New Afrikan. I do not consider myself an American citizen. I consider myself a New Afrikan citizen. You may have heard the term the Republic of New Afrika mentioned by the judge -- or if you haven't, you will. The Republic of New Afrika is the name given our Nation by a group of Black people who came together in 1968 and who decided to declare ourselves free and independent of the United States. Like the British colonializers, the American colonializers, which they are, because we are a people whose total wealth is controlled. When i say we, i'm talking about Black, New Afrikan people in America, all the wealth that we produce is totally controlled by the big businessmen that run and control the United States of America would have you believe that i am a criminal, that we are all criminals. That just isn't so. I am a New Afrikan soldier, and we have an absolute right to fight for our freedom. That is a human right. That is not a right that your oppressor gives you. That is not a right that you have to ask or beg for. Like all people who want to be free, what is necessary to exercise that right is to stand up like men and women and exercise it. If it calls for fighting, then we fight.

They say that we have come together for the purpose of criminal activity to further some kind of racketeering purpose. They have us indicted on charges that were originally devised for the purpose of organized crime. They are doing that to hide the real reason for what is going on. The real reason that i and many other Black people in this country are fighting and why many people support this just struggle of ours.

Most of us here at this table have long years, long history in political activity and political affiliations. My activities goes back around twenty years. All of my adult life, i am 38 years old now. That is no secret to the government. I have been a target of the government for a long time. I was part of the Black Panther Party way back in 1968 when we tried to organize in the community certain programs that would help bring Black people up non-violently. The same thing happened. We were attacked and accused of many things, framed of many things. I was part of, i don't know if any of you would remember, the New York Panther 21 conspiracy case that went on for about two or three years and eventually we were found not guilty. But by then, i had been forced underground because they weren't able to grab me on the day they grabbed most everyone else, and because they had put out threats for my life and they had swore to kill me whenever they found me, i did what was logical. I hid. But i didn't just run.

I continued to fight. I continued to build.

The good programs that we were trying to institute within the Black Panther Party, breakfast for children, free clothing drives, free food give-a-ways, they were successful for a while until they were infiltrated by the u.s. government under a program called COINTELPRO and destroyed. They brought in agents, they paid informers, paid people to come in and lie and say people were doing things they weren't doing. They caused conflict within the structures and had people fighting each other and they were successful in just about destroying the Black Panther Party.

But there were many, many people that came through the Black Panther Party who they weren't able to destroy or capture and frame. A number of those people became part of an underground army. Some people call them members of the Black Liberation Army, Black Liberation Forces, many differing names, but in fact, they are soldiers fighting for the liberation and self-determination of the New Afrikan Nation.

(below) Happy Birthday to Abu & Tupac, ca '85.
(left) Tupac, Mouse, Yaki at Sekou and Tupac's birthday, ca '85.
Even though Sekou was incarcerated, we always celebrated his birthday (June 17) along with Tupac's (June 16).

(below left) Sekou, released in 2015, finally meeting his granddaughters Valencia and Nyasia.

(below right) Sekou spoke at UCLA after his release, the campus where Black Panthers John Huggins and Bunchy Carter were murdered. A tribute to them was erected at UCLA.

In the name of Allah the Beneficent the Merciful!

Yafe'u Akinyele Fula ibn Sekou Odinga
He lived fully and fast, never one to linger
Son, brother, friend and expectant father
Those he loved he truly loved, others he didn't bother

Kadafi was my son who I loved very much, but who I knew very little. He was born in 1977 while I was underground fighting for the establishment and liberation of the New Afrikan Nation. The first four years of his life we spent a lot of time together. We had a strong loving father-son relationship.. That relationship was interrupted with my capture in 1981 by u.s. colonial forces

HAPPY
BIRTHDAY
YAFEU

LOVE
ABU

Nightcap
Dixie Dunnaway

Summertree PRESS

In the name of Allah

My Dear Son
  Peace, how are you? I hope you and your mom are doing fine.
  I got you and Tupoc's letters today and they made me very happy. I was real surprised to get the letter from Tupoc. Tell him I said Peace and I send my love.

THE 80S - *Pied Piper*

Tupac was the Pied Piper wherever he lived, no matter which housing project or tenement whether it was the Bronx, Harlem, or Washington Heights. We lived all over New York. In every recess of every neighborhood, Tupac was a leader. Yaki was right there by Tupac's side with total adoration, absorbing it all. They were both perfectly placed to embrace the eruption of hip-hop as the Bronx was center stage and they were totally immersed in the new sound.

Tupac studied and dissected this new style of storytelling. I believe this is why so many of the fans loved his music. Each verse of his songs told a story. He told his own story; he told his mother's story; he told the Panthers' story, but as a whole, he told the story of a people. He had been taught from birth that our successes and talents must be used for the liberation and enrichment of black people. He wasn't just grooving to the beat. Though a disciple of many great elders, Tupac was formulating a plan of success. He couldn't wait to get out into the world to implement his plan and show us he was capable.

He was a genius with words because his mother made him read constantly. He was exposed to music of all genres: jazz, rock 'n roll, blues, r&b/soul, doo-wop, reggae, folk, songs of protest, songs of revolution. But first he had to master the methodology. It came naturally to him and he perfected it as he intersected daily with the cultural heartbeat of Harlem during its most prolific Black power movement. The streets were filled with poets, corner orators, musicians, and bright souls all day, every day. Tupac's creative juices were tantalized on the streets of New York City. It was his mentors, his elders, and his teachers who tendered the philosophies and courage necessary to be an instrument of change.

We focused the passion of our sons to make them understand their talents must be used beyond creative or monetary cravings. They had an obligation to address the suffering of others through their art. The great Rollo May laid it out in *The Courage to Create*—to have the courage to leap into the unknown despite overwhelming feelings of despair. We encouraged our sons to be unconventional architects of change despite the conditions we faced. For Tupac, who was exposed to the written word through books, social activism, speeches and music at such an early age, this came naturally.

It was not a coincidence he became the lyrical genius of hip-hop. His place in hip-hop was cemented instantaneously, not just because of his phenomenal lyrical style, but his message of social reform and unification was a perfect fit to the blistering denunciations of America's inner cities being played out in daily life.

Tupac was a young disciple from birth and he shared the torch of resistance with Yaki. The ordinary exploits of children growing up during the 70s were obscured from these young men as the star of revolution loomed over their heads guiding them to their final destination. There was no time for fantasy, but they

The Pied Piper and crew; Yaki at top left, Tupac on the mic. Bronx, ca '85.

dreamed of a world free of discrimination and fear. Tupac knew firsthand this discrimination and fear from having lived through the targeting of political activists by domestic surveillance programs resulting in incarceration, exile, and death of his village. New York was the hub of the Black power movement intersecting revolutionary black conscious and poetry ripping to music by groups such as the Last Poets, Poor Righteous Teachers, Gil Scott Heron and the Midnight Band—beloved Bilal Sunni-Ali. These were the original conscious rappers giving birth to a new generation of social/political commentators—hip-hop. Tupac and Yaki were in the melting pot of beats, DJs, and all the legends of the day—the boogie down BRONX. It was the home of salsa, Johnny Colon, and Héctor Lavoe blasting in East Harlem, while the tempos of John Coltrane resonated from 125th Street—Harlem on my Mind.

Tupac and Yaki were soaking it all in, with a healthy dose of the B-boy, DJ, boombox culture. He lived in the epicenter of hip-hop origins—Washington Heights, Woodycrest Avenue in the Bronx, 7th Avenue in Harlem. For them, life was now the boom box, the human beat box, and breakdancing. It was Grandmaster Flash, Kool Moe Dee, Sugar Hill Gang, Curtis Blow, and Slick Rick. I mean they played Rappers Delight and Slick Rick's song, "Children's Story," so much, to this day when I hear these songs I still pause for a moment and smile! "Like a Jungle Sometimes Make Me Wonder How I Keep From Going Under." I can still see the eager young faces of the young neighborhood kids as he assembled them in formation to play and then later on, to make recordings. But back then, never did we imagine Tupac would become this legendary prolific MC, the only solo rapper to enter the Rock and Roll Hall of Fame.

He inherently understood the essence of hip-hop because he lived it on the front lines with staunch human rights advocates whose personal sacrifices framed those beats and verses. The sounds of gunshots, refrigerators with no food, hot summers with open fire hydrants, acupuncture at the Lincoln Detox

Hospital where addicts were detoxed off heroin, spending hours riding the subway to get to the jail to see your father. He knew the potential of this art form as a way to empower the youth, unite the streets, and make some money to survive. The spoken word came easy for Tupac. Truth and liberation went hand-in-hand and so the magic of his music wove a mesmerizing spell by simply ascribing the lessons learned in his youth to a beat.

Nothing prepared him for his future career more than the emphasis placed in our homes on education. We were educated and informed about the true historical disparities in America as it relates to Black people and we passed this knowledge to the children in our homes. We read poetry by Langston Hughes and Maya Angelou, plays by Lorraine Hansberry. In 1983, Tupac played Travis in Hansberry's *A Raisin in the Sun* with the 127th Street Ensemble, the Harlem theater group. We were inspired with her insight, particularly her line, "Eventually it comes to you: the thing that makes you exceptional, if you are at all, is inevitably that which must also make you lonely."

So it was for Tupac. As a young revolutionary artist searching for his own identity, Tupac was inspired by the Harlem Renaissance whose influence is still apparent in Harlem. Tupac was a voracious reader and so the teachings of scholars like James Baldwin became gospel, "The obligation of anyone who thinks of himself as responsible is to examine society and try to change it and to fight it no matter what the risk."

Knowledge was power and we transferred this power to the children in the form of books. Reading was a requirement, every day. We read about other liberation struggles, books by Frantz Fanon, novels by Richard Wright, *1984* by George Orwell, the words of Langston Hughes. Harlem was our laboratory with the dynamic cultural, political, and social uprisings of the 60s and 70s of which we gleefully participated. We would walk the streets of 125th Street, always stopping at the Lewis Michaux Harlem bookstore where there were street orators and political discussions going on right in front. We would pick Tupac up to read the sign over the bookstore:

Lewis Michaux inside his bookstore.

127th STREET REPERTORY ENSEMBLE
PERFORMING 4 GREAT DRAMATIC WORKS
SALUTING THE 10th ANNIVERSARY OF HARLEM WEEK

Day	Date	Time	Play		PERFORMING COMPANY	
FRI	August 10	8:00	RAISIN ***		Jerome Bates	LeCora Prince
SAT	August 11	3:00	RAISIN **		Torrence Bates	Ira Richardson
SAT	August 11	8:00	RAISIN ***(*)		Regenald Bennet	Rhonda Russell
SUN	August 12	3:00	RAISIN		Michael Brown	Rita Scott
SUN	August 12	7:30	RAISIN		Helen Butler	Ed Sewer III
MON	August 13	8:00	EQUUS *		Tanya Collington	(Tupac Shakur)
FRI	August 17	8:00	ZOOMAN		Tredessa Dalton	Jim Shorts
SAT	August 18	3:00	ZOOMAN **		Donna Dunstan	Levy Simon Jr.
SAT	August 18	8:00	ZOOMAN ****		Mervin Evertz	Donna Smith
MON	August 20	8:00	EQUUS		Milton Evertz	Hazel Smith
TUE	August 21	8:00	EQUUS		Kevin Fahey	Donald Taylor
THUR	August 23	8:00	ZOOMAN		Minnie Gentry	Bahni Turpin
FRI	August 24	8:00	ZOOMAN		Synthia Henry	Kevin Valentine
SAT	August 25	3:00	ZOOMAN **		Miles Jay	Greg Wallace
SAT	August 25	8:00	ZOOMAN		Bruce Jenkins	Charles Watts
					Carolyn Jenkins	Robert Williams
					(Scott LeSane)	Ron Williams
SUN	August 26	3:00	RAISIN		Linwood Lloyd	
SUN	August 26	7:30	RAISIN		Jacquelyn Lynch	
MON	August 27	8:00	RAISIN		Lola Louis	
					Tomi McNeil	
THUR	August 30	8:00	MOON		Wanda Moore	
FRI	August 31	8:00	MOON *		Tommy Newman	
SAT	Sept. 1	3:00	MOON **		William Plant	
SAT	Sept. 1	8:00	MOON			

smile now

HARLEM MONTH THEATRE FESTIVAL 84

127th STREET REPERTORY ENSEMBLE
the Theatre Company of the 21st Century
ERNIE McCLINTOCK, Dir.

18th SEASON

ZOOMAN AND THE SIGN — CHARLES FULLER

RAISIN IN THE SUN — LORRAINE HANSBERRY
Minnie Gentry GUEST ARTIST

EQUUS — PETER SHAFFER

MOON ON A RAINBOW SHAWL — ERROL JOHN

In Repertory

AUGUST 10 –thru– SEPTEMBER 1, 1984
WALDEN THEATRE 88th STREET & CENTRAL PARK WEST
General admission $8.
Reservations\info: 289 5900

cry later

Smile Now, Cry Later was one of Tupac's tattoos.
Poster and clipping from program where Tupac played Travis in A Raisin in the Sun.

Cheryl Davila and Yaki at an outdoor concert in Newark.

Tupac and Yaki spent summers together every year. During the school year, they were together always on the weekend. Katari was also often with us. We would gather up everyone and drive to one of the NJ shore spots and have a grand time.

Tupac would go to camp with Yaki and they would have a ball. It was important to me that Tupac had a chance to be just a boy, a kid having fun, and he did that quite a lot during these visits. He would oftentimes call me to come get him whether we were living in New York or New Jersey, or they were living in Maryland. He and Yaki were always making plans to hang out and I was their personal driver.

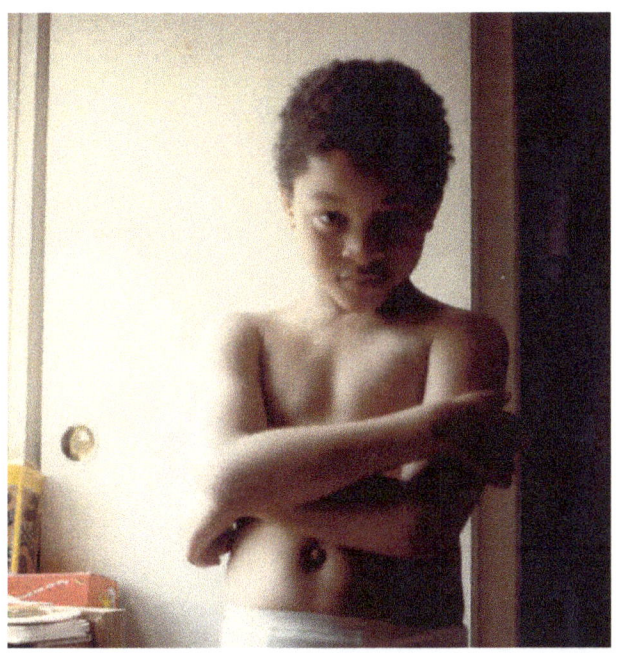

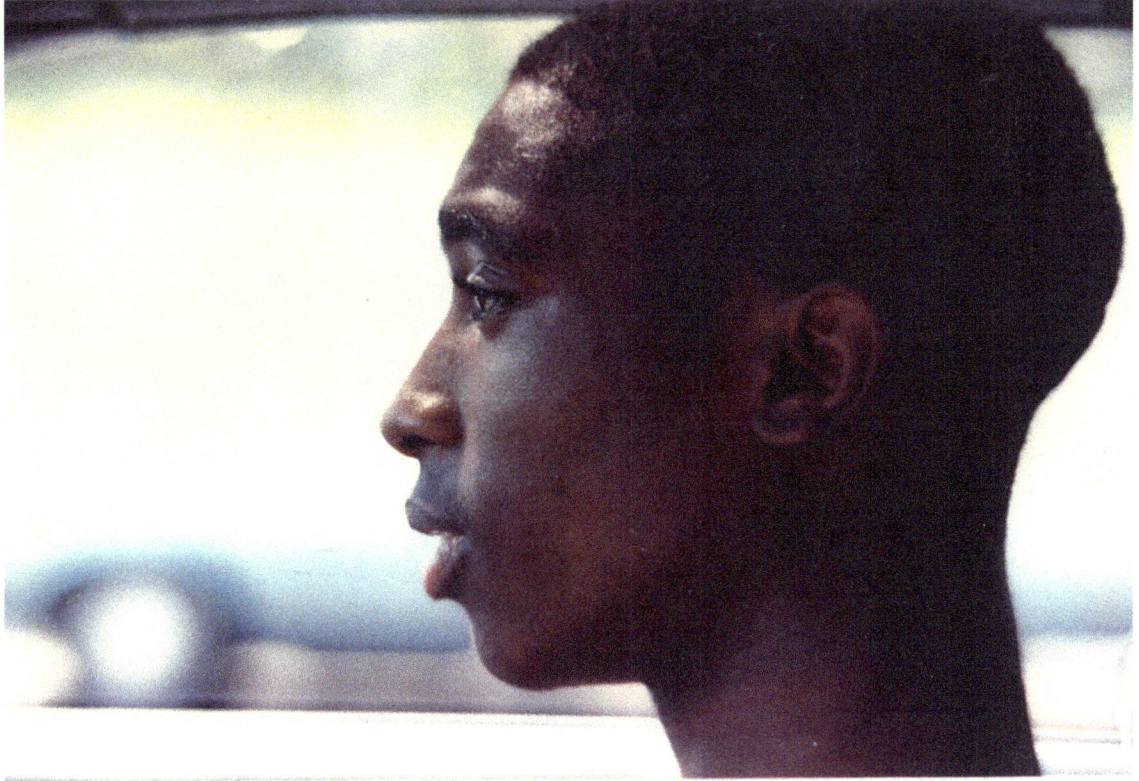

(previous spared) A good day at the Jersey shore with Katari, Yaki, Badalia, Tupac, and Cheryl Davila.

(clockwise from top left) Sekou's sons, Malik and Anoche holding their baby brother, and Yaki and Tupac. Malik and Anoche are twins and Yaki's half-brothers, Bronx.

Yaki enjoying some pudding.

Soapy Yaki, East Orange, NJ

Yaki and Muhammed Odinga, Yaki's half-brother, Harlem, ca '85.

Tupac posing in front of my Camaro IROC. He loved to pose in front of the cars, ca '86, Bronx.

(top) Sharonda, Yaki, Tupac, East Orange, NJ.

(left) Yaki asleep in my Camaro.

(below) Katari, Marc Smith (Yaki's cousin) and Yaki horsing around in the Bronx as they watched Tupac pose in front of my Camaro, ca '86.

(opposite) Yaki sporting his then-fashionable high-top fade.
(top) Yaki, Sharonda (all grown up, Tupac not chasing her), Tupac, and Cheryl on their way to a Queen Latifah concert.
(bottom) Pac loaded up and ready to go, Baltimore.

Digital Underground

*L*ife was once again overwhelming for Afeni. It was 1988 and they were living in Baltimore. Tupac was sent out to California on a bus with a bag of chicken wings to live with Ashaki, Geronimo's wife. I was devastated. In New York, he was insulated and protected from the danger of the streets as he was always under a watchful eye. In the Bay area, unsupervised and away from his family, he went through the dangerous rites of passage without his protectors present. The streets become the mother and father. Fortunately, the hustlers and dealers quickly recognized his talents and discouraged him from selling drugs.

Tupac met Leila Steinberg who took him to TNT Records and from there to Digital Underground in the early 90s. He went from roadie to on stage as a back-up dancer and then onto their albums as a rapper. The release of his debut single "Trapped" and then the follow-up "I Get Around" were immediately successful.

When Digital Underground went on tour with Big Daddy Kane, we had front row seats at Symphony Hall, Newark, NJ. Yaki could barely contain his excitement seeing his brother perform on stage! He was

jumping up and down in the front row and I caught a picture of Tupac smiling right at Yaki. Tupac's performance forced Yaki to consider Tupac as not just his big brother, but now also as a star. Yet Yaki remained unfazed with his brother's newfound celebrity status. Unlike so many quick to revel in idolatry, Yaki was simply happy to see him on stage and Tupac was still just his big brother; nothing had changed.

When he left Digital Underground at the end of 1990, his solo career was launched. The release of his first solo album *2Pacalypse Now* in 1991 included his hit song "Brenda's Got a Baby." His second album *Strictly 4 My N.I.G.G.A.Z...* was released in February, 1993.

(left) Tupac performing with Digital Underground, looking at Yaki and me, front row, Symphony Hall, Newark, NJ.

(opposite, clockwise from top left) Tupac with Digital Underground, Newark, NJ with headliner Big Daddy Kane.

Tupac throwing confetti on Yaki in the front row, Yaki was so excited, he couldn't keep still!

Shock G and me, House of Blues, ca '05.

Tupac's first business card.

EVOLUTION OF THE OUTLAWZ

*The most courageous act is still
to think for yourself.*
~ Coco Chanel

In the beginning around 1994, Yaki, Malcolm, and Katari transitioned from Thoroughheads to Dramacydal. They performed as Dramacydal on *Me Against the World*.

"Runnin' from tha Police," featuring Yaki, Tupac, Biggie, and Stretch, was intended for Tupac's album *Thug Life* but Interscope Records came under heavy criticism at the time for promotion of so-called gangsta rap so it was shelved. Then it was supposed to go on *Me Against the World*. The shooting of the Atlanta off-duty cops in 1993 was followed by Tupac being shot at the Quad Studios in 1994 during his criminal trial for a sexual assault charge. The song was finally released on the *One Million Strong* compilation album. It is one of the few collaborations of Biggie and Tupac. All of these young men are deceased, cut down in the prime of their lives. It was one of my favorite songs, especially Yaki's verse.

Strong themes of police encounters and protest permeate this song. "Runnin' from tha Police" was as much a cry of defiance and resistance against their exploitation as it was a reclamation of their dignity. The verse haunts me to this day. Runnin' from the police in Montclair, NJ was sport to Yaki as he fell deeper and deeper into the spell of the streets, surrounded by other young boys growing up without fathers.

At one point, during Tupac's incarceration, Yaki and Fatal were going to also record under the names Fatal and Felony. In fact, the infamous Death Row paper contract dated September 16, 1995, signed while Tupac was still in prison, outlined compensation and points:

> THUG LIFE - $250,000
> DRAMACYDAL - $200,000
> FATAL & FELONY - $200,000

Even while incarcerated, trying to secure bail for his freedom, Tupac still demanded the record label also sign his crew.

Yaki and Fatal (RIP) always had more of an edge in their music delivery. Fatal was so very talented but so tormented and undisciplined. I was the one who brought him to visit Tupac at Clinton Prison. In the visiting room, Tupac told Fatal, "Let me hear you spit." Fatal spit some rhymes and Tupac liked what he heard. But Fatal proved problematic and ended up being expelled from the group and sent back to NJ in the summer of 1996. Fatal was a source of deep disappointment, unable to overcome his own demons.

When Tupac was released from jail and he started his Death Row days, the members of Dramacydal were referred to as "lil' homies" by Suge. Yaki resented Suge referring to them as Tupac's lil' homies or "Tupac's children."

Yaki never backed down expressing his opinion to his brother and rejected any notions of subservience. He had his own mind, his own identity. Growing up, he quickly became Tupac's counterpart–never one to bite his tongue. He lived up to the meaning of his name Yafeu, which means bold. Tupac always had a sparkle in his eyes when they performed on stage together. He was proud of Yaki. Yaki was a leader, very opinionated and considered himself a equal to Tupac, not an underling. Rebellion was in his blood. Yaki was the heart and soul of the group, tall, handsome, charismatic. Every inch of his 6'2" frame exuded boldness and intimidation, especially to short people with larceny in their hearts.

One day Yaki told Tupac, "We ain't no lil' homies. We're Outlawz." And so it was.

The renaming of the Outlawz was as much a political move as it was a creative one. Yaki's protestation to Tupac about not being "lil' homies" was an extension of a fierce understanding they were living lives of displacement, without the benefit or protection of laws, justice, or equality. Tupac had studied and applied the concept of "outlaw" which codified the awareness and dedication of purpose which was his mission.

When Tupac came up with the monikers for the group members, he asked me to do the research. He always thought in the context of global relationships and as such, he considered only international figures. Tupac was determined to maintain a global connection through his music. An urban guerrilla group, the Tupamaros of Uruguay–named after the Peruvian Túpac Amarus–inspired his creative juices constantly. He identified with leaders who exerted power, even at the risk of being dictatorial.

Assigning these particular monikers was no coincidence. Tupac studied these notorious figures and attempted to match the character and physical attributes–always prodding and motivating them to expand their horizons beyond mere rap. Katari was named after Fidel Castro. Malcolm was named after the president of Uganda Idi Amin, stylized into E.D.I. Mean. Fatal's name was from Saddam Hussein. Yaki was named after Muammar Gaddafi. Mutah was named for Napoleon Bonaparte.

Storm as a solo act and The Outlawz were to be the first ones Tupac signed to Makaveli Records. The expectation was The Outlawz would emerge as disciples of their mentor with an allegiance to the principles Tupac lived and died for. Tupac never wanted them to sign with Death Row. So what did they do after Yaki and Tupac's deaths? Against my wishes, against the wishes of elders with a vested interest in seeing the legacy of Tupac and Yaki continue, The Outlawz signed with Death Row.

In an effort to maintain the integrity of Tupac's legacy and wishes Hafiz Farid contacted, among others, the Kenny Gamble of Gamble and Huff, Philadelphia International Records. Gamble, a powerhouse in the music industry, had relationships with BMG and outlined a strategy to secure a great deal for The Outlawz. The Outlawz, poised for solid backing and investment, rejected all deals, soon conjuring a reputation of being more of a liability rather than an asset.

The Outlawz signed with independent Koch Records, ending up in litigation with both Koch and Death Row Records. Death Row was to be their death knell. After they signed with Death Row, all previous deals were off the table, as the chaos and confusion surrounding this label was considered too libelous.

Application of the readings of Niccolo Machiavelli's *The Prince* was both theater and enlightenment for Tupac. The precepts of maintaining power and control of one's domain, as recounted in The Prince were intriguing. Tupac knew he had no army, no real soldiers on his team. A prince who has no army but knows the art of war will prevail over a strong army. So he armed his disciples with the art of war - knowledge - preparation - dedication to the struggle. "The streets is military…. You gotta be a soldier…."

But The Outlawz failed to understand their responsibility to carry on the legacy of Tupac and Yaki. They were not just members of a rap group. They were foot soldiers now charged to carry on the teachings of their mentor. They had a responsibility to collaborate with the heirs of both warriors to truly understand how that legacy should endure. That did not happen. "Too busy trippin' off his shine…"

Rappers are often disconnected from the true historical roots of hip-hop. Once you disconnect from the roots, the tree will die. Tupac was about the business of re-building the community. The hip-hop scene has become a maze of shuffling troubadours bowing down to scripted degenerate behavior that is both destructive and demeaning in order to make a grab for the almighty dollar.

Tupac never intended for his legacy to merely advance careers. In hours upon hours of marathon political education (PE) lectures, Tupac outlined plans for the future, as he always saw death around the corner. He envisioned a new world order using music as a unifier to promote dignity and respect among all people - nation building through the framework of hip-hop culture. He understood his responsibility as an artist as practiced by his predecessors–Lorraine Hansberry, Paul Robeson, Langston Hughes, and Gil Scott Heron–all who clearly understood that they are not in the business of entertainment, but rather they are in the business of communication. The ultimate goal was then–and always will be–Liberation. He was embracing hip-hop culture as a vehicle to carry on the torch of nation building and self-determination.

Codes were violated, loyalties betrayed. The Outlawz were being held to the task of carrying on the political visions and dedication of re-building communities, as outlined by Tupac. They failed to do so, rapidly devolving into self-serving minstrels in the rapidly deteriorating minstrel show known today as hip-hop.

After Yaki's murder as I made the arrangements for his funeral, I thought about Emmett Till's mother. In Mississippi in 1955, Mamie Till made the agonizing decision to leave the casket open of her mutilated son. She wanted the world to witness what was done to her beloved child by southern racists. As I thought about that, I also thought about Yaki's verse from the *One Million Strong* album's song "Runnin'":

> **IF I DIE, BURY ME A G,**
> **OPEN CASKET ON THEM BASTARDS**
> **SO THEY ALL REMEMBER ME**
> **WITH MY VEST ON MY CHEST**
> **THUG LIFE**

I made the decision to have the casket open as the damage done by the assassin's bullet was so profound. I said, "Son, yes, we are going to open casket on them bastards so they all remember you."

But unlike Emmett Till, the enemy was not from without, the enemy was from within. The very people my family lifted up rewarded me with a bullet to my beloved son.

FataL-N-FeLany
"Hollywood, N.J."

1. Brothers N Armz (w/ 2PAC)
2. ~~tha Authorized~~
3. A Kriminals Dynasty
* 4. Dis Aint Living
5. Between Us
6. If we could Trade Places
7. Running From Da PoPo
8. I'll make u famous
* 9. Kriple Connectionz
10. Fatal Attractionz (solo)
* 11. TrueLiez
* 12. Blocklife - PopLife
13.
14. Mama Use 2 Say

(clockwise from top) Track list for Yaki and Katari's planned recording

One Million Strong album cover

Katari, Malcolm, Jamala, and Yaki sitting on my BMW, Bronx, '95

We are outlaws because of the anti-African economico-politico-socio-spiritual circumstances in capitalistic and racist America! People of color have historically been and still are excluded from complete freedom, justice, equality and economic participation in this predominately European-American country. Racism has been institutionized and continues to be propagated as a smokescreen to keep the masses confused and divided. We recognize that the real struggle is between the oppressive and exploitative "Haves" and the oppressed and exploited "Have-nots"! We are outlaws because in order to achieve all that we will, we must operate outside of this corrupt system and we have no problem in consciously doing so as a continuous act of rebellion and open defiance against our enemies!

Excerpts from *The Outlaw Manifesto*, written by Kahlil M. Salaam.

The Outlaw Soldier lives by honor and respect on all levels! The True Outlaw Soldier understands that the words "Outlaw Soldier" has a very high and honorable meaning(s)! If circumstances demands of the Outlaw Soldier that he/she sacrifices his/her life for our struggle, so be it! Once again, it is very imperative for all of us to fully understand/comprehend that "Outlaw" is a "Politically-Conscious/Aware Soldier" and not an "Apolitical (Unconscious/Unaware) gangster or criminal"!

The "Outlaw Soldier" must be tested! He/she must never forget that, first, we must practice true brotherhood and sisterhood and then loyalty and love to one another on all levels! This will eventually grow into an unbreakable and impenetratable unity, which won't be infiltrated and also unmatchable power to control our own family destiny!

Our purpose is a "Just (Righteous)" struggle! Our overall aim is to build-up our communities through our own efforts and initiatives. We must nurture, provide for and teach our babies and youth, feed the hungry, unite broken families and create new families who are completely "loyal" to us. We intend to also take care of and highly respect our "Elders". We definitely intend on making every effort to raise the political consciousness/awareness of our communities wherever we are!

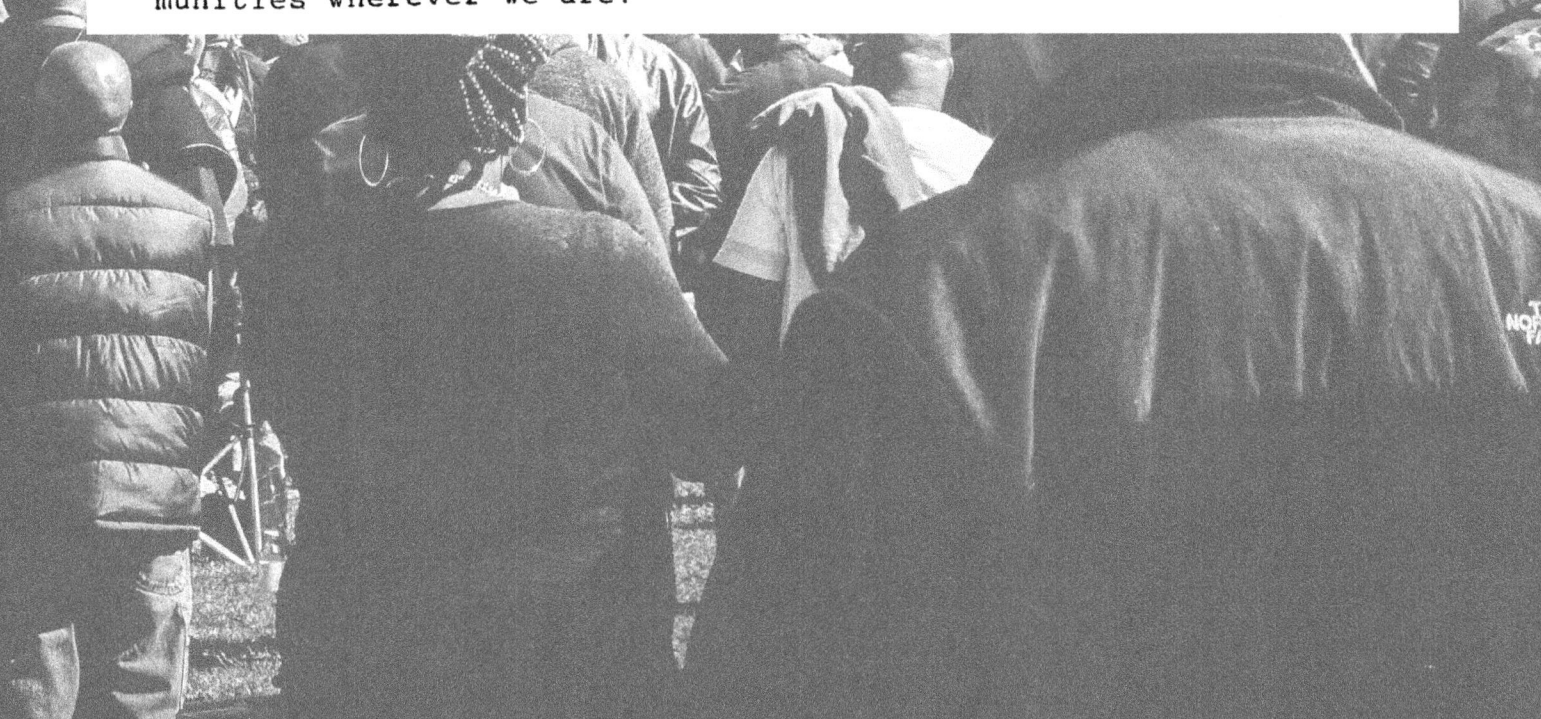

The Big Picture

Tupac holding book written by Sundiata Acoli, '92.

After the release of *2Pacalypse Now*, Tupac's career took off fast. His first starring role was in the movie *Juice* in 1992. Prior to that, he appeared in a cameo with Digital Underground in the movie *Nothing But Trouble* singing "All Around The World, Same Song" in 1991.

I remember all of us going to the movie to watch him in *Juice* where he starred as a streetwise troubled kid doing what Tupac always did—organize and lead. His role as Bishop was no different than his real-life persona, only this time his violent screen portrayal drew cries from family members in the audience. One of his cousins yelled at the screen, "C'mon Pac! Why you gonna shoot him? Don't do that!" We were so proud of him.

Over the years, when any of his movies would have its release, Tupac would fly back to New York to celebrate with family and friends. He was always accompanied by a crew of folks eager to get a good home-cooked meal from Tupac's Aunt Gloria.

Elders, like Aba Shakur, father of Zayd and Lumumba Shakur, were present to honor Tupac's achievements. Aba was the patriarch of the Shakur clan, a proud and dignified elder, respected globally for his love and dedication to human rights.

His next film, *Poetic Justice* in 1993, showed Tupac's more sensitive side as Lucky the mailman. He was excited to be co-starring with Janet

Celebrating the release of Juice with family and friends.
(top row) Tupac, a family friend, Afeni, Aba Shakur, Sekyiwa, Shadia Odinga. (bottom row) Ali Bey Hassan, Anoche Odinga.

Jackson and to have a role of a black man with a job providing for himself and his family. It was on the set of this film Tupac met the great Maya Angelou who soothingly put loving arms around Tupac during one of his notorious fits of anger. She reminded him what his ancestors went through on slave ships and auction blocks. She told him, "It was all for you to be where you are today." This brought Tupac to tears, and had the effect of immediately quelling one of his explosive emotional outbursts.

Above the Rim, also filmed in 1993, was the turning point for Tupac. The decisions he made during the filming of this movie were haphazard with grave consequences. Tupac was riding the wave of success in the fall of 1993 when he began shooting *Above The Rim*. The successful release of his album *Strictly 4 My Niggaz...* and his movie with Janet Jackson, *Poetic Justice*, made Tupac an attractive target.

During the filming of *Above the Rim*, Tupac was charged with sexual assault in real life. He was associating with many unsavory characters during this time. His godmother Crooksie made desperate attempts to get messages to Tupac by trying to contact him at the filming location on 140th Street, New York. The characters depicted in most of his movies—drug dealers, gangsters, and petty hustlers—were all stereotypical roles with subliminal messages that romanticized drugs and gang banging. As Tupac played these roles, his on- and off-screen personas seemed to merge as his character Birdie attracted real life hustlers and predators. Tupac was ill-equipped to regulate them both professionally and personally. He had crossed over into their world while playing a fictionalized character, one that he despised in real life, but one whose flirtations with danger became increasingly difficult to leave on set. It was the proverbial Faustian bargain—compromising his moral integrity through association with the devils of darkness. The beginning of the devil's pact.

The *Above the Rim* soundtrack was released by Death Row/Interscope records and it was only the third Death Row album to reach the charts. It is historical because it was a so-called gangsta rap label yet it came into mainstream prominence. The soundtrack stayed on Billboard's charts for ten weeks.

Many artists were introduced on this soundtrack, which included the birth of a new style known as G-Funk. This album was stocked with tracks from Snoop, Tha Dogg Pound, and other West Coast artists and it was the first to feature R&B artists like SWV and Jodeci. This was ironic considering that it was a movie about New York hustlers in Harlem and it did not feature a single current New York rapper (with the exception of Wu and Treach's guest verses) and the star of the film, Tupac, was not even signed to Death Row Records. Behind the scenes, the management contracts of artists with Uptown Entertainment and Andre Harrell were being taken over now by Death Row Records and Suge Knight. The rivalry between East Coast and West Coast was already cementing and Tupac, by not considering the implications of these events, was central to the drama soon to have a perilous impact on his life.

The die was cast as Tupac was now immersed in the East Coast-West Coast rivalry. Appearing to have promoted Death Row (West Coast) artists on the soundtrack for a New York film was felt by many to be a slap in the face of the East Coast—his home base. In 1995 at the Source Awards, Death Row won best motion picture soundtrack for *Above the Rim* and on that night, Suge Knight challenged hip hop artists to join Death Row in New York City, which only fueled fires of resentment and feelings of betrayal toward Tupac.

Tupac's only song on the soundtrack, "Pour Out A Little Liquor", was recorded with his group Thug Life. There was always a special message in his songs for the brothers locked up. That's Yaki in the Thug Life video, sitting on the sofa around 15 years old, under the watchful eye of Tupac. He wanted Sekou to see and be assured he was looking out for his son. The irony of it all. The only Tupac song on the soundtrack received much criticism for not including more East Coast rappers. Yet, the song was about honor and responsibility that must be shouldered, despite loss and death. And so it was with Tupac, a study in contradictions.

Getting to' down for my niggaz in the Pen, yo
Your son's gettin' big and strong
And I love him like one of my own
'Til you come home...

There was no male figure in Yaki's life that protected him like Tupac. He truly loved Yaki like a son and always wanted him around so he could watch over him. There is no doubt in my mind the premeditated murder of Yaki would never have happened had Tupac lived. Yaki's death was carried out by a family of cowards with no character. The shooter told witnesses days before he was going to kill Yafeu and on November 10, 1996 that's exactly what he did.

Tupac's work ethic was unstoppable. He was signed to Death Row Records and still filming movies. In 1996, he shot both *Gridlock'd* and *Gang Related*. When we spoke, I emphasized to Tupac that Death Row would recoup from the soundtracks but that all revenue generated from his movie performance was his money. When his money started coming in from his movie contracts, we were able to start truly building Euphanasia, Tupac's production company.

All of the money prior to his film contracts was from his pocket as it relates to building the business. We were considered to be Death Row's "employees" which meant there were constant "mistakes" made in our compensation. Vendors were not paid, lawyers were not paid, production costs were always being undermined. Any money Tupac requested for video production, movie/project development or family expenses, if allocated at all, was routinely recouped without benefit of audits or statements. The *Gang Related* checks didn't come until August 1996. That didn't leave much time for Tupac.

Tupac was exhausted. From the day he was bailed out from the NY prison, he hit the ground running on a mission to prove to the world he was not a rapist. For someone raised by women and a staunch defender of women's rights, the conviction did more trauma to his soul than any assassin's bullet.

Two movies in one year, plus two chart-breaking albums. He was running on empty. I remember getting calls from security, Frank Alexander or Kevin Hackey, attempting to wake Tupac up for the 6:00 a.m. cast calls for the *Gridlock'd* set, having only left the recording studio a few hours earlier. Nobody liked the assignment of waking Tupac up under these circumstances.

(opposite) Tupac in between filming Above The Rim and Poetic Justice.
(below) Afeni, Tupac, Sekyiwa after Poetic Justice.

Bullet, another crime film where Tupac plays a stereotypical bad guy drug dealer, was written by Bruce Rubenstein with Mickey Rourke as his co-star. Tupac and Mickey's friendship was forged during the filming of *Bullet*. It was posthumously released in 1996, a month after Tupac's murder. This meant he had three films released in 1996.

He was dogged by the bad guy images, roles that Hollywood producers offered in limitless supply. They were literally blowing up our phone at the Euphanasia office with movie roles for the drug addict, thug, criminal gangster. Tupac was wary of these roles but he equated the cash with independence so he could continue building his empire and take care of his family.

(opposite pg) Tony Davila, Scott Lesane, Tupac, Jamala Lesane.

(top) Tupac with phone, Scott, and Tupac's roadie Charles Fuller (Man Man) standing in front of my white Saab, NYC.

(left) Tupac holding his nephew Malik.

(pg 99, clockwise from top left)

Tupac and Yaki.

Tupac and Sekyiwa.

Tupac and Afeni.

Yaki and his half-brother Malik Odinga.

(pg 100) top: Sekyiwa, Tony Davila, Katari, Scott, Jamala; bottom: Yaki, Tupac, neighbor, '93, Washington Heights, NYC

(left top) Tupac and Tom Cox, who was a father figure to Tupac and an inspiration to us all.

(right bottom) Tupac showing off his new threads.

(left bottom) Tupac on his cell phone in front of my Saab, NYC.

Picture Me Rollin'

*E*very time Tupac got a new car, he was so proud. He especially enjoyed passing me the keys to go for a ride. As a young boy, he loved when Yaki and I came to get him in whichever car I was driving at the time. Cars meant freedom and movement for his restless soul.

As he grew up, Tupac and I shared a special moment together with each car he acquired, whether it was a BMW, Bentley, Jaguar, Hummer, or Mercedes because he knew how much I loved nice cars. I was no longer the chauffeur chaperoning Tupac and Yaki all over town in my car. Now he was the boss and it filled him with immense pride.

But the reason Pac acquired a few of these cars was because our office, Euphanasia, through Tupac's attorney, requested an accounting audit from Death Row of Tupac's finances. Death Row would ignore these requests and give us no accounting, just more gifts.

In 1995, Tupac purchased a new silver BMW 840 in New Jersey. He loved being able to tell me, "Yas, I just bought a new Beemer, go pick it up and bring it to me!" I drove it to him in Atlanta.

He always waiting by the door for me to come pick him up. When he was a boy, it was, "Yas, come get me...please!"

When he became the boss, it was still, "Yas, come get me...please!" He knew I would be there.

One night, in the wee hours around 2:00 a.m., I get a call from Tupac. Tupac had his Hummer at a club and the valet attendant couldn't get the truck in gear. I said "Pac why are you calling me? Nobody else there can put a truck in reverse but me?"

He said "Absolutely right! Nobody here knows a damn thing about a car like you do. You were probably born in a car. In fact, I promise when you die, I will make sure you are buried in a car!"

I couldn't stop laughing while I got dressed and came to his rescue in those early morning hours. That was nothing new for me. I loved him so.

(opposite pg) Gary Tyler, Malcolm Tyler, Katari, Asania Tyehimba, Jamala Lesane, Tupac, Yaki, and a very pregnant Sekyiwa.

(top) Me in Tupac's Hummer.

(bottom) Tupac's Jaguar, leased for him by Death Row.

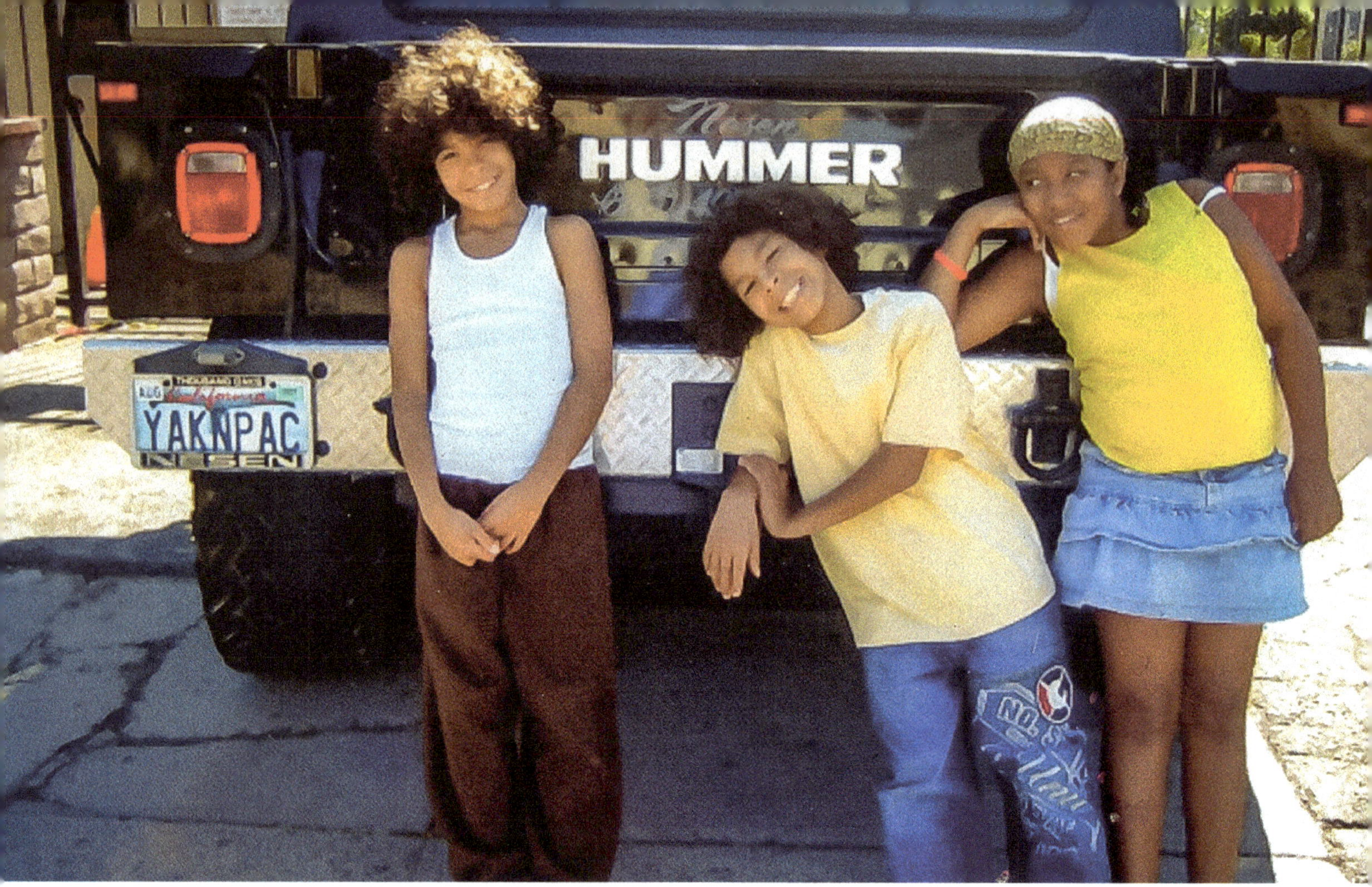
HUMMER
YAKNPAC

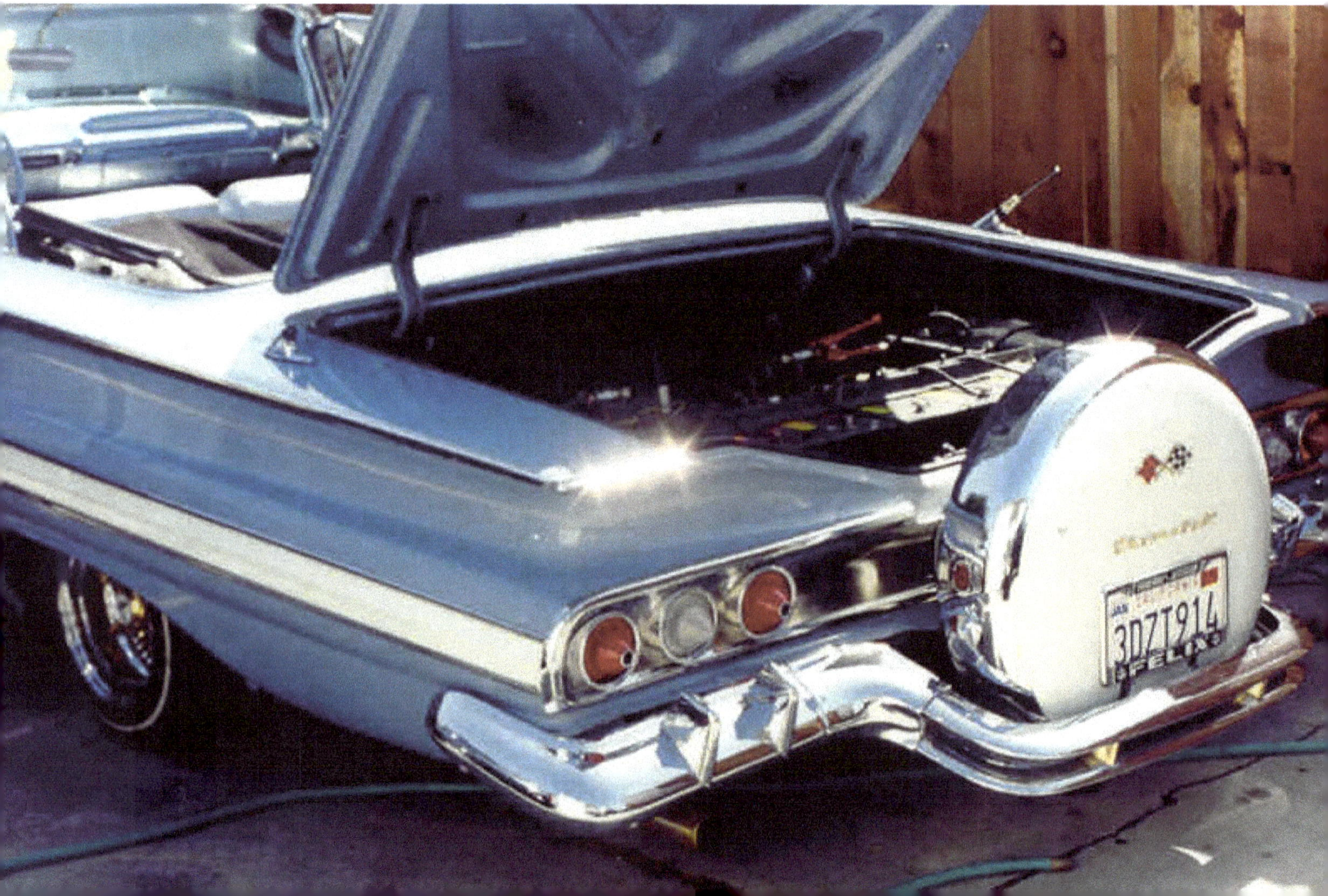
3D7T914

(opposite pg top) Isaac and Elijah Bell and Yaki's daughter Nyasia Key posing next to the Hummer. Note the license plate!

(opposite pg bottom) Tupac's 1964 Chevrolet Impala.

(this page top) Tupac and Afeni in Tupac's brand-new BMW that I drove down to Georgia from New Jersey.

(this page bottom) Kidada's beloved dachshund, Penny, hanging out in the backseat of the Hummer.

ATLANTA - *Lock, Stock, and Barrel*

*...I WILL TRAIN MYSELF NEVER TO HURT OR ALLOW
OTHERS TO HARM MY BLACK BROTHERS AND SISTERS...
~ BLACK CHILD'S PLEDGE*

Tupac stood on the shoulders of great African American scholars, writers, activists, and revolutionaries. It was an entire village of strong men and women from every religion, race, ethnicity who confronted America's racist history. More than anything, the defense of the community against wanton brutality was a fundamental lesson learned at an early age. The shooting incident of two off-duty Atlanta cops in 1993 elicited a collective shudder in our hearts. While his street cred soared, so did the resentment from many law enforcement agencies.

On the day of the shooting, Tupac and his crew were coming back from Clark University in Atlanta. Yaki was in the car behind them. It seems Yaki was always in the car behind, never in Pac's car. Tupac, always the protector. Pac saw what he thought were two white men harassing a black man. As a defender of the underdog, he had strong feelings about bullying. To drive by and not stop would have gone against every ideal, every code of conduct, and every lesson from every noble man and woman who whispered in his ear growing up. They said, "You have a responsibility to your people: never cause them any harm, never turn your back on them, and do everything in your power to protect the people." Nothing in Tupac's DNA would let him just ride past. Afterwards, many of us wished he had done just that. At the very least, I wish there had been a voice of reason to subdue the temper of our strong-willed native son.

As the story goes, he got out of the car, asked what was going on, and was told by the off-duty officers to mind his business and get back in the car. An argument ensued and the two officers were shot. It was later determined that they were off-duty, intoxicated, and with weapons stolen from an evidence locker. Charges were dropped against Tupac, but we knew it was not over. The two cops ended up suing his estate and settled after his death.

Yaki and Tupac were both surrounded by people in touch with their soul's purpose. Tupac understood at a very early age, during very turbulent times, the nation was in crisis and his life had purpose. Yaki was learning, in training, under the tutelage of his beloved brother. They both needed the guidance and wisdom of their fathers, men from the same ilk and passion, fearless yet strategic. Left to their own devices, with no one to fill the voids, no guiding hands to interpret the world, temper their anger, their survival became interdependent on each other. From that fateful day in Atlanta, Tupac had a permanent target on his back.

Had he learned and lived the Way of the Warriors, he would have approached like a fox, fought like a lion, and disappeared like the birds.

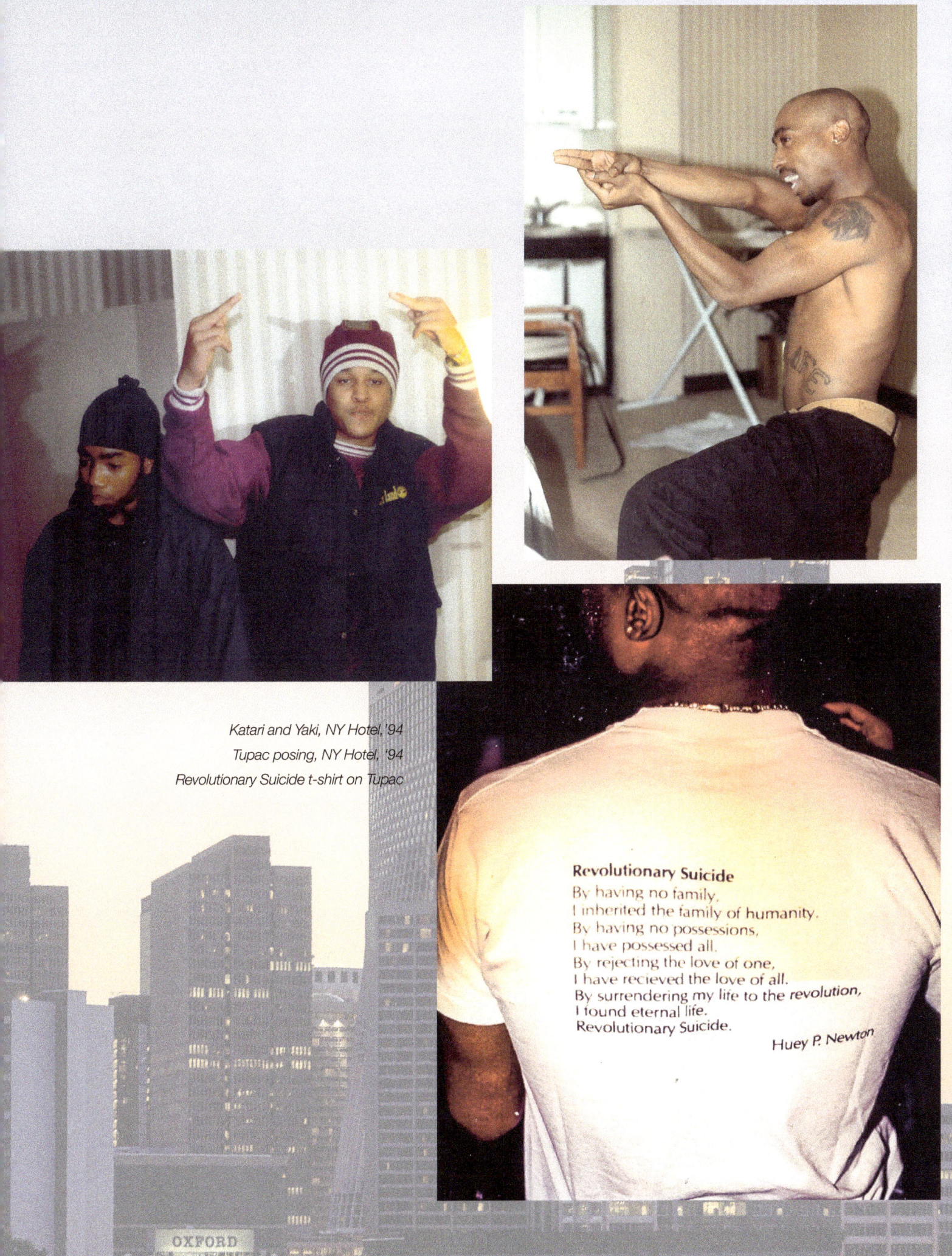

Katari and Yaki, NY Hotel, '94
Tupac posing, NY Hotel, '94
Revolutionary Suicide t-shirt on Tupac

These photos are from Tupac's home in Atlanta, ca '94.

(opposite pg, clockwise from top left)
Lyrics for Thugz Mansion, written by Yaki.
Yaki and Malcolm.
Sekyiwa, Afeni, and Helena at Sekyiwa's baby shower.
Katari, Mopreme, Afeni, Yaki, Sekyiwa, and Billy Lesane.

(top, this pg) Tupac and Yaki.
(left, from left to right) Mopreme, Malcolm, Tupac, Katari, and Yaki.
(bottom, from left to right) Tupac, Katari, Aunt Gloria (wearing THUG LIFE shirt), Sekyiwa, Afeni, Yaki, and Mopreme.

TRIAL- *The Setup*

*E*ighteen days after the arrest for shooting the two off-duty Atlanta cops, Tupac was arrested and charged with sexual assault in November 1993. There was never a question in our minds that Tupac was innocent. But with the rumors of the unsavory characters hanging around, no one was all that surprised when he wound up with criminal charges. Tupac would never cause physical harm to any woman, nor would he allow anyone in his presence to do so. He had stopped his car in Atlanta to assist a stranger, a black man he perceived was being beat up by two white men in civilian clothes. It would have been against his nature to witness a brother being roughed up by two white men and not intervene. Similarly, had he witnessed the abuse or assault of a black woman in his presence, he would have surely intervened to stop it.

Many warned Tupac not to continue his associations with certain individuals just as he had been warned not to sign with Death Row Records during his incarceration. Despite testimony there were other men in that room at the Parker Meridien hotel, Tupac and his roadie Charles Fuller were the only ones charged. Everyone else just disappeared. Even though his DNA test came back inconclusive during the trial, he was still convicted of slightly lesser charge of sexual assault.

Tupac was raised around revolutionaries and hustlers that lived by codes. The brothers on the block that ran the numbers and hustled in the streets were symbiotically connected to the BPP. But Tupac was insulated from the gangster and drug dealing culture that preyed upon people because that culture was contained. There was always an ethos, a code imposed in Harlem by old gangsters like Bumpy Johnson, who defied Dutch Schultz's mafia control of the numbers rackets and drug sales in Harlem in the 1950s. Historically and traditionally, there were always men in the community that protected the people. After the BPP was dismantled by the FBI's COINTELPRO, the infrastructure that imposed codes of conduct in the streets was shattered. With the Panthers out of the picture and no longer a presence, the community was overtaken by drug dealers previously chased out of town by Panthers. There were no longer cadres of men snatching the stashes of the drug dealers' heroin and pouring it in the sewer or advocating for the welfare of women and children. There was now a culture of predatory economics that openly preyed upon the people. The crack epidemic of the 80s destroyed an entire generation with the birth of crack babies. The ethos of caring for your community first and foremost was replaced by a Get Rich or Die Tryin' ethos. The game had changed.

Tupac made the mistake of thinking this New Jack culture of gangsters could become formidable allies in his quest to transform and rebuild the community. He was dead wrong. The drug dealers and street hustlers from his youth had adhered to some codes of conduct. But by the mid-80s, Black men in the new game, this Get Rich or Die Tryin' hustle, did not share in his consciousness and perceived him to be a threat because he could not be contained. His nagging sense of feeling vulnerable and unprotected led him to make deadly miscalculations

We were standing inside the court during the trial watching the press outside amassing, waiting for Tupac to emerge. I said, "Pac, were going to walk straight to the car, you have no comments, no reactions. Be careful because they are going to try and get you to respond." He agreed.

As soon as we stepped outside the courthouse, they rushed him like a pack of wild animals. In spite of our talk just seconds before, Tupac started spitting at them to get them to back up.

On the night of the shooting at Quad Studios, we had spent the day in court. Tupac's pager was blowing

Portia Kirkland, Tupac, and me leaving the court during the trial as press and camera crews aggressively rushed us from all sides.

up with calls from various individuals pressing him over and over as to what time he was coming to the studio. They were calling every 20 minutes. This lasted for hours until Tupac, out of desperation, threw his pager at me, screaming, "What the fuck is wrong with these people? I told them what time I was coming. I'm in fucking court!!" But the calls continued throughout the day, most everyone calling wanting to know when he would get to Quad. From the first moment he agreed to go there, he had a gut feeling that things weren't right. He ignored this feeling and later that night, he was shot in the lobby of Quad Studios.

🎲

I remember coming to Bellevue Hospital to break the news to Tupac of the conviction as he lay in bed riddled with gunshots. It tore my heart to have to tell him. It was an intense time as Tupac was reeling from the ultimate betrayal of being shot five times and now was convicted of sexual assault.

When he was released from the hospital, he holed up to recuperate at Jasmine Guy's home. It was there that contemplation of taking his own life was discussed with family members. I was livid!!

I said, "Pac, you got four years. You will be out in two or three. If you remember, I did 18 months when I was found in civil contempt and survived. You're not looking at 20 years. You will be out on bail pending appeal in a few months. We got you on this. Professor Ogletree already has good grounds for the appeal."

I will never forget his response. "Yas, it's not the time; it's the dehumanization…surrender to being a real slave now? *Yes'sir, boss; no'sir, boss.* I'd rather be dead than surrender my dignity and my respect to a bunch of racist KKK guards who will all be waiting to give me their ass to kiss."

I understood. Here was a warrior, a soldier, never surrendered, never a POW, never a shackled slave. It had nothing to do with fear. It had everything to do with honor. Like a Samurai warrior ready to die before dishonor, like a caged animal contemplating his escape routes, he was delirious with anger. Going

TO: THE BLACK COMMUNITY, THE AMERICAN PEOPLE, FANS, UNDERGROUND RAILROAD, NEW YORK RACIST PRESS:

2PAC IS NO RAPIST!!

Recent events involving the arrest of **2PAC** Shakur on charges of sodomy in New York is an outrage and attempt by the New York Police Department to silence a young man whose brilliant and politically conscious rap style is seen as a threat by the white power structure. The subsequent tirade of **vicious lies** and prejudicial newspaper coverage that followed his arrest were carefully orchestrated by the New York City Police Department, whose maniacal tendencies to engage in illegal and immoral behavior have been well documented in the recent corruption hearings. In view of the irresponsible news reporting, outright lies and attempt to portray **2PAC** as some mad monster on the loose only demonstrates the pathetic collusion of the press with the NYPD to deny him a fair trial. **2PAC IS NO RAPIST!!** - He is a revolutionary conscious young black man who was raised to love, honor and respect his people. We know had **2PAC** not chosen through his lyrics to expose AMERICA's violence and the violence it has perpetrated against black people, then he would have never been targeted and set up. We are the survivors of **COINTELPRO!!** - We know how the system targets, sets up and eliminates its most vocal critics.

Since the press chooses not to engage in honest and objective news reporting we have undertaken to present the truth to the people. We will not sit by idly while the media destroys yet another successful young black man through character assassination and cesspool reporting and thus destroying the presumption of innocence. Since the media has chosen to conduct itself as **"propaganda whores"** around **2PACs** case, we will, during the course of this trial, put the facts and truths out there for the people to decide who is the real victim. Malcolm said that America will always try to make the victim look like the criminal and the criminal look like the victim. By labeling all rappers as so-called "gansta rappers" and blaming them for the violence in our communities America once again absolves itself of any responsibility in creating this culture of violence that impacts on all our lives. Through his music **2PAC** has always rapped about the self-hatred, self-degradation and fratricide warning our youth not to become the agents of our own destruction!! Why then has he come under attack ? Know the facts so you can decide who is telling the truth!!

THE CHARGES OF SODOMY AGAINST 2PAC AND HIS ROAD MANAGER, CHARLES FULLER SHOULD BE DISMISSED!!

Strategic evidence destroyed by the New York City Police Department included the erasing of explicit voice mail messages left at the Parker Meridian Hotel by the so called victim/groupie. These messages were very important as they illustrated her character and mental state at the time as well as disputing the reasons why she came to the hotel on the evening of November 18, 1993. This outright destruction of crucial pieces of evidence by Detective Flaherty of the New York City Police Department was disclosed to **2PACs** attorney by Mr. McDonough, Director of Hotel Security at the Parker Meridian Hotel. It defies reason that a woman who engaged in oral sex with **2PAC** in a Manhattan club four days prior to the sodomy charge, would in the privacy of a hotel have to be forcibly convinced to similarly conduct herself. Before **2PAC** had even been arraigned this well known groupie had retained a civil lawyer to sue for money and fulfill her wicked scheme for financial gain.

This was no date rape, this is no feminist cause célèbre, this is no brutal act of rape. - This is a setup!! **2PACs** fans have remained loyal because they know him to be incapable of this most heinous crime --His love and devotion to women are deeply rooted in his music and his life. From his recent hit song '**Keep Ya Head Up**':

....and since we all came from a woman,
   got our name from a woman,
....and our game from a women,
   wonder why we take from our women,
....why we rape our women,
....Do we hate our women?

By charging **2PAC** with the most heinous of crimes the NYPD thought they could silence **2PAC** by destroying his career and credibility in the eyes of the public. **NOTHING COULD BE FURTHER FROM THE TRUTH!!** Much of **2PACS** music is devoted to the plight of young black women, and for that reason is loved and revered by his fans, most of whom are sisters!! In falsely attacking him the NYPD underestimated the consciousness of black people in 1993, and their ability to discern who the real criminals are. After realizing their so-called victim was nothing more than a lowly groupie whose credibility will be destroyed in court the police concocted an even more bizarre story that **2PAC** was a child molester!! Knowing the potential damage a mere accusation would have, the NYPD called upon the New York dailys and t.v. networks to further smear the brothers name with this filth!! When it became clear these new charges were fabricated by the NYPD the media offered not even an apology or retraction!! It is no wonder **2PAC** is angry at the media for participating in the conspiracy to destroy his career!!

ATLANTA CASE

The New York charges came on the heels of an incident in Atlanta where 2 off duty gun wielding, drunken Atlanta police officers were shot after attacking **2PAC's** entourage and smashing the windows in his car. As with the New York media, the Atlanta press has printed only the police version, which was in direct contrast to the numerous eye witness accounts. During pre-trial hearings the truth came out!! The cops were off-duty, drunk and never identified themselves as police! Even more damaging was their admission that they used guns in the altercation stolen from the Atlanta police department evidence room!! They have been charged with aggravated assault and disciplined by their superiors for getting caught in this very compromising position. **2PAC** is also charged with aggrevated assault and we are awaiting the findings of the grand jury. We thank all who have shown their love and support and encourage you to come to court and demand hands off **2PAC and CHARLES FULLER!! Demand media and press accountability!!** Come to Court February 18, 111 Centre St., 9th floor, Judge Fitzgerald. Stop the media bashing of black entertainers!! Most of all KEEP YA HEAD UP!!

2 PAC IS NO RAPIST!! CHARLES FULLER IS NO RAPIST!! WE WILL WIN!!

Flyer in support of Tupac and Charles Fuller during the trial.

Tupac appearing in court for sentencing, his hand was bandaged after having been shot at Quad Studios.

Illustration courtesy of Marilyn Church.

to jail was one thing but going to jail innocent, convicted of assaulting a woman, was so heinous, so opposite to everything he stood for.

Jasmine nursed Tupac while he seriously contemplated surrender or going out in a blaze of bullets. My devotion to his life was unwavering. Winking and nodding and biting my tongue in order to keep the peace was never my way, even if it meant defying loved ones. I was prepared to fight for his life, even when discussions of suicide rendered the landscape even darker and more dismal. There was no way around the inevitable. Life must go on, if for no other reason than to prove his innocence. I was outraged that there was serious discussion of suicide as an option. It was cowardly and I made my feelings known at every turn.

Yaki passing on bad habits to dear friend Portia Kirkland - notice the bird! ca '94.

Clinton Prison—*The Ordeal*

We set up shop near Clinton Prison located in Dannemora, New York. We lived in hotels and incurred expenses flying visitors in and out of this upstate town even though money was tight. Organizing the business visits and family visits required careful coordination—especially the ladies' visits. The plan was to keep him out of his cell by scheduling as many visits as possible. In between the visits, Tupac spent many hours in isolation, reading, studying, and plotting the future.

Tupac wrote a script titled *Live 2 Tell* while incarcerated. During our visits, he would surreptitiously pass his drafts to me in the visiting room. I sent him the book *How to Write a Screenplay* by Syd Field and together, we learned how to write a screenplay. I had to learn how to type in the screenplay format. This was 1995, before the days of widespread email and being able to send a file digitally. I would print out and mail the typed copies along with the handwritten pages back to Tupac. He was so excited to be creating this story. It kept his mind occupied and gave him hope. By the time he was released on bail in October 1995, *Live 2 Tell* was a completed first draft.

In the fall of 1995, Tupac was interviewed by filmmaker Ken Peters. At the time of the interview, (Tupac's only video interview while incarcerated at Clinton), we were all still reeling with devastation and disbelief at the murder of 11-year-old Robert "Yummy" Sandifer on the south side of Chicago in September of 1994. Born to a teenage drug-addicted mother and with his father in jail, Yummy became a killer and then was killed by the time he was 11 years old. I remember reading the article to Tupac, "...as a baby he was burned and beaten," and then murdered by his own gang members for killing the wrong 14-year-old girl. We were so sad yet outraged. Brutality against children was always hard to bear but this particular incident tortured his soul.

Tupac never got over Yummy's death, especially as his love for children was so profound. During a concert in Milwaukee at the Mecca Arena on September 13, 1994, he confronted members of the Gangster Disciples thought to be responsible for Yummy's death. During the show he stopped and called for a moment of silence for Yummy. He was outraged when these alleged gangsters shouted "thug life" during the performance. Tupac felt they got it twisted and started cussing them out calling them cowards for killing Yummy threatening, "You better stop killing those babies or else I'll murder you myself."

What followed was far from a moment of silence. It became pure bedlam—a shootout and riot. Yet, in spite of the chaos, the mothers and girls from the community sent letters to Tupac thanking him. His

HOW CAN THESE PEOPLE BE TALKING ABOUT THEY SO REAL AND DON'T CARE ABOUT OUR COMMUNITY?

connection was always to the women. He felt vindicated by the mothers.

Especially riveting in this interview at prison is where Tupac speaks to the lack of support for the community from rappers: "How can these people be talking about they so real and don't care about our community? Listen to what they saying. Don't just bob your head to the beat. Peep the game. Listen to what I am saying and hold us accountable for it."

Every fiber of his being was for the advancement of the people. But even with all the courage and love for the people in his heart, Tupac overlooked some important lessons. Behaving impulsively and emotionally will not achieve victories. Fearlessness was his badge of honor, but unfortunately his youthful blunders were magnified before the world to judge. He had been at war since he was a tiny fetus but now this war required strategy and not just raw emotion. With all his mentors locked up, the missteps were huge. Miscalculation of his strengths, allies, and exposure to many frivolous dangers left him unprotected, off-balance. He needed the wise counsel of those faithful to his mission and not the flatterers who flocked in abundance ready to pass the joint and sip the wine.

During Tupac's incarceration at Clinton, I did what I always did. I handled his business, I protected him, and I counseled him as best I could but he was still overwhelmed with the circumstances. Tupac's appeal lawyer was Charles "Tree" Ogletree, a noted Harvard law professor. Tree assured us, based upon his review of the case, there were numerous legal errors during the trial. Several jurors were dismissed after expressing disgust for Tupac and his music. The prosecution was caught withholding evidence during the trial. With these issues and several others, bail pending appeal was anticipated.

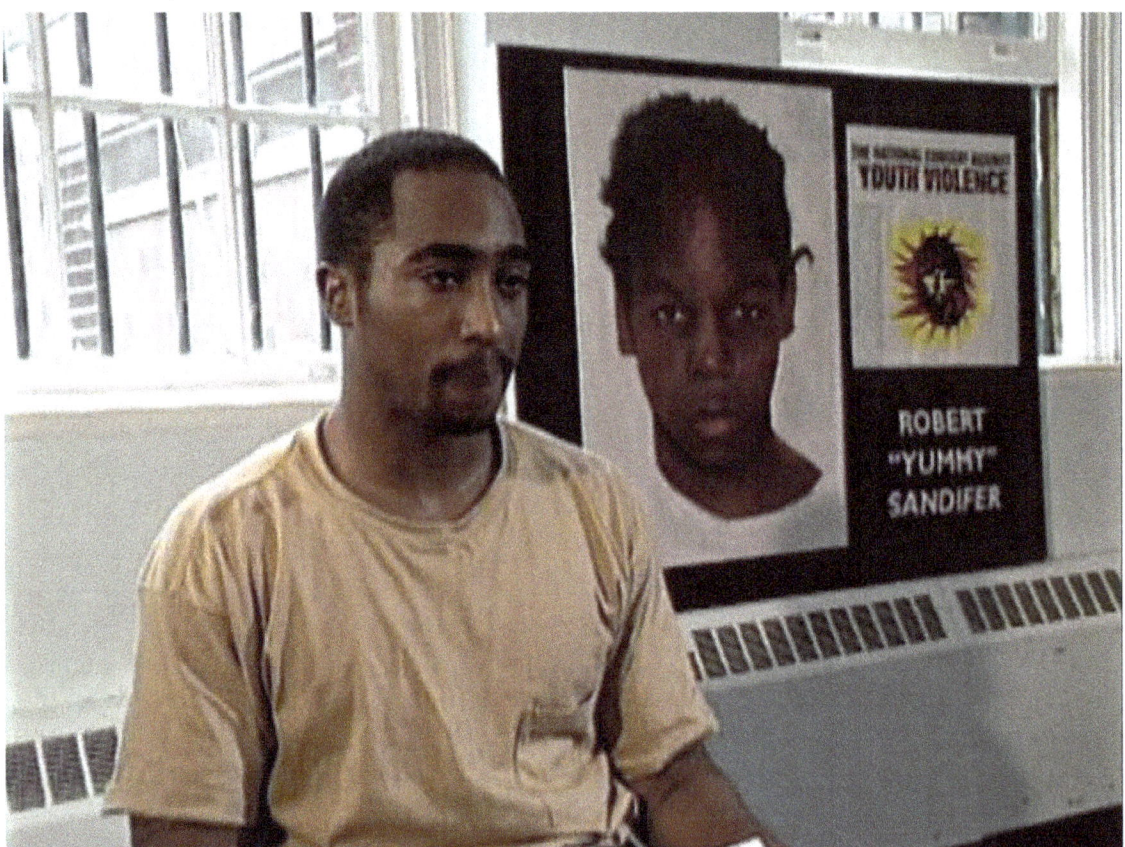

Photo from Tupac's prison interview with filmmaker Ken Peters.

Big Syke and Bogart holding vigil outside the prison.

Tree emphasized to Tupac that the basis of this appeal revolved around the presumption of his guilt that dominated his trial, rather than the proper position of presumption of innocence.

The Presumption of Guilt, a documentary film by Hafiz Farid and Shelley Grodner Seidenstein, was based on Charles Ogletree's 2010 book of the same name.

Through this, Tupac really needed someone to act as intermediary with his appeal lawyer Charles Ogletree and the record labels so they could negotiate a proper deal for bail and recording contracts. It was a complicated deal between Interscope Records with a guaranty by Atlantic Recordings for the 1.4 million dollar bail. Interscope guaranteed to reimburse Atlantic Recordings via the infamous three-page handwritten contract Tupac signed in jail with Death Row.

At that point, I'd never heard of Death Row Records. I surmised, based on the scores of people visiting Tupac, pleading that he not sign with them, that it was a bad deal. But Tupac was desperate to get out of jail. His family was dependent on him financially. He would have signed with Lucifer to get back to freedom, and by all accounts that is exactly what he did.

Driving back and forth to Clinton for his signatures on various documents, I was filled with such joy yet apprehension. Tupac was coming home but the warning signs of this new alliance with Death Row Records were ominous and hard to ignore.

Finally, on October 11, 1995, bail was granted pending the Appeal of Conviction by Judge Silverman. The vigil had started outside the prison weeks earlier with The Outlawz and many others who came and left. Of course, the admin at Clinton took their sweet time processing him out.

These Polaroids were taken in Clinton Prison.
(top left) Tupac, Kastro, and me.
(bottom left) Me, Tupac, and Jasmine Guy.
(top right) Yaki and Tupac.
(middle) Yaki and Tupac.
(bottom right) Tupac and his father Billy Garland.

Tupac was released October 12, 1995. I will never forget when he walked out of those gates. I said, "Pac, give thanks, son, give thanks."

The first thing Tupac wanted was a joint, a glass of Alizé, and his money. The pictures capture the minutes following his release. I had all that ready and some new threads, too.

He had come to the hotel with a bag of paperwork and other miscellaneous items. The last official repudiation of the ball and chains of the past eight months in prison—he wanted no paperwork that would remind him of his former slave status. He threw it on the bed. "Burn it, I don't care what you do with it. Just be ready when I call. I got plans."

Along with the Alizé, I handed him a briefcase with his money stacked. He was very, very happy to have his money. The Outlawz and Syke handed him a blunt. For the first time in a long time, he smiled that deep infectious Tupac smile. He called his mom. And then he got in the limo that was waiting for him. It took him and Syke to the airport, and he boarded the private jet headed to Cali and went straight into the studio.

(left) Tupac smiling that famous smile holding his glass of Alizé as we celebrated his freedom in a hotel room waiting for his plane to arrive.

(above left and right) In fresh threads, heading back to Cali with Big Syke.

(next page) Tupac and Syke on the plane to California; you can see me taking this picture in the very middle.

DEATH ROW - *Dark Forces*

....All around the mulberry bush the monkey chased the weasel.
The monkey thought it all was in fun
Pop goes the weasel.......

Upon Tupac's release from jail in October 1995, he went straight to the Death Row's recording studios to record his next album. *All Eyez on Me*, his fourth album, was released by Death Row Records in February 1996. Everyone who worked with Tupac was astounded at his whirlwind pace. It took only four months to conceive, record, and release this album. It was a testimonial to Tupac's genius and lyrical prowess. He spent his time at Clinton prison contemplating the songs that best illuminate the pain and betrayals of the past year—and it was all poured into this epic work. It sold 566,000 copies the first week. Tupac made history because it was the first double-length hip-hop solo studio album. This was his second album to hit number one on both the Billboard 200 and the Top R&B/Hip-Hop Album charts.

His third album, *Me Against the World*, debuted at No. 1 on the Billboard 200 after its release on March 14, 1995. He poured his heart out in *Me Against the World*. It was typical Pac—brutally honest, baring his heart and soul—So Many Tears. All of his heroes were either in jail or dead: Geronimo Pratt, Mutulu Shakur, Lumumba Shakur, Sekou Odinga. This was not a glorifying of death. This was social commentary on a culture of violence that infected everyone and one in which he truly saw Death Around the Corner.

When *Me Against the World* was released in 1995, he earned the dubious honor of being the first artist to have an album debut as No. 1 while serving time in prison. With the release and success of *All Eyez on Me*, rap's first double-length solo album, his quest for vindication and truth was still unfulfilled, but set to explode in his next and final album *Makaveli the Don Killuminati—The 7 Day Theory*.

The cover of Makaveli that depicted Tupac on the cross set off a hailstorm of religious angst. How dare he presume to be Jesus Christ the Savior! I remember when he showed me the mock-up created by artist Ronald "Riskie Forever" Brent. I said, "They really are going to crucify you now."

I discouraged him at first, but then we talked and I understood. Tupac felt a deep sense of betrayal having been shot. He naively thought the people understood he was fighting for their rights and would never put him in harm's way. The torment of false conviction, imprisonment, and media crucifixion filled his heart with an unbearable sense of abandonment. He was, after all, the knight for the oppressed but now felt he had symbolically been nailed to the cross.

I wanted to protect him from further harm, but I knew his destiny was already scripted. He would never back down from an opportunity to advance the black liberation struggle and expose the hypocrisy of Christianity that separated itself from the black condition and its true meaning. This album was to be Tupac's swan song, his final revolutionary act of depicting the true gospel of Jesus Christ, resurrected symbolically in his image. Like Jesus Christ, Tupac believed he was a voice for the voiceless, the oppressed.

Original mock-up of Makaveli album, created by Ronald "Riskie Forever" Brent.

He understood that the work of Jesus was the work of human liberation but that traditional Christian theology was a manipulation of religious zealots and Illuminati myth to control the masses.

I found my book, *A Black Theology of Liberation* by James Cone, a noted black Christian theologian, and explored its content with Tupac. James Cone wrote, "There can be no theology of the gospel which does not arise from an oppressed community." James Cone was a brilliant theologian who was the first to explain the cross was the lynching tree of the oppressed.

I also read this passage to Tupac from Cone's book, "…the movement for black liberation is the very work of God." It is what his heart and soul already knew and now Tupac felt vindicated fully rejecting American white theology and all of its hypocrisy and betrayal of the true spirit of Christianity. It was a rejection of a practice of white supremacy that sanctioned genocide, wiped out the original Indian population, and enslaved indigenous people all over the globe.

He was elated as we analyzed these passages. He was by no means a Bible-carrying, suit-wearing, church-going Christian but I could sense his joy to have James Cone, a scholar, validate Jesus Christ in a revolutionary context.

Tupac never departed from the true scripture—all people have a right to live in peace free from domination and persecution.

Makaveli was posthumously released November 5, 1996, 22 days after his death and only five days before the murder of Yafeu.

TUPAC NEVER DEPARTED FROM THE TRUE SCRIPTURE—ALL PEOPLE HAVE A RIGHT TO LIVE IN PEACE FREE FROM DOMINATION AND PERSECUTION.

By distorting the essence of his life, an image of Tupac Amaru has been created to characterize and portray him as just another iconic thug. In distorting his life, the focus is shifted away from a culturally enriched life, intent on building collective economic wealth, and left to become a demeaning Who Shot Pac minstrel show, perpetrated disgracefully by people who have demeaned his sacrifices.

The travesty is when Tupac died so did his dream of building progressive community programs in every inner city. He was always calling for unity and community centers in the neighborhoods to deal with everyday issues—education, employment, mental health, police brutality, drugs, prisons, sexual exploitation, women's rights, loneliness, mentors for kids, shelters for kids. He knew because he remembered his own sense of frustration as a child feeling abandoned by the movement, and his family traumatized by the sacrifices they made in pursuit of a more just world.

He had a vision for a bigger better world that was quashed with the Quad shooting and conviction for sexual assault in November of 1994. But his time in jail allowed him to revive and refocus his vision and upon his release from jail, he was burning brighter than ever before.

The spirit of Tupac Amaru is deeply rooted in the global indigenous resistance movements. His legacy, now associated with music industry moguls and movie ratings, stands in sharp contrast to his true spirit. He lived and died believing all people have the right to live with dignity and in control of their own destinies. Wary of corporate domination and exploitation of his artistry, since the inception of his career, he sought to implement frameworks that maximized his independence and control of his legacy. Self determination was in his DNA. The last thing Tupac would have wanted was his legacy controlled by music moguls with a perverted fidelity to exploitation of the artist. This was contrary to every fiber of his being. Incredulous that his dreams of ownership and independence from corporate domination have all been quashed. His escape route from the plantation, while meticulously planned in life, was cut short by an assassin's bullet in 1996. The bounty hunters have returned the corpse to the plantation. The Crows remain vigilant over the carcass. The prophet must not resurrect; there will be no more escapes.

(left) Yaki under the Thug Mansion neon at Tupac's home in California.

(right) My negatives from The Outlawz 1995 show at Club 662 in Las Vegas.

EUPHANASIA- *The Road Back*

COME NOT BETWEEN THE
DRAGON AND HIS WRATH.
~ KING LEAR

During all this time, I continued handling his business, faxes, and updates from his attorney regarding his legal cases. Staying in touch with Tupac was problematic as he moved from hotel to hotel using various names, including one of his favorite ones "Welcome Home Homie".

Sometime around Christmas 1995, he called me and told me to pack my things to get ready for the next level. He was ready to build his media empire. It was what we talked about while he was in jail: his own company. Tupac's mindset was always about ownership and controlling one's destiny. He was an early disciple to concepts of community control and learned from the sacrifices of many dedicated men and women that the building of a nation required choosing courage over comfort. He was on the front lines with us supporting labor movements, prisoners' rights movements, health care movements, rent strikes, and building conversion to tenant ownership through sweat equity. He was taught throughout his life there can be no self determination without self sufficiency….OWNERSHIP.

I left New Jersey at the end of January 1996. I hitched my BMW on a U-Haul and loaded my doggie Louie. I stopped in Atlanta to pick up Tupac's cousin Philip Cox and Tupac's boxes from his mother. I was finally a California Dreamer.

Euphanasia Incorporated was Tupac's company. I incorporated the company in Delaware and we were excited to be shareholders. At first, Tupac wanted to name the company Euthanasia. It was his notion of the right to choose when to live or die. I said, "No, Tupac. People will think we are Dr. Kevorkian's death squad." So I did some research and played around with the name and suggested Euphanasia—derived from the word euphoria—a feeling of well-being.

The 2Pac Fan Club was not just a fan club but a service club for the fans. While in jail, he had grown, transitioning from taking risks to making every minute count.

I told Pac that when I spoke to the fans, they all expressed the turmoil of their lives and how his music had helped them overcome difficult days. Among the many things we were planning, there were plans for a 24-hour hotline so fans could call for support when in crisis. If they needed to talk, we put them in touch with outreach services and referrals, whether health crisis, domestic violence, or homelessness shelters. He understood the trauma of his generation—self-esteem, powerlessness, hopelessness, and poverty. Tupac wanted to model the Fan Club as not just a typical fan club but rather have it as a service-oriented agency—like Bronx Legal Services—that would coordinate with other outreach and intervention organizations to build infrastructures primarily for at-risk kids.

Euphanasia was to be the parent company for his record label Makaveli Records, a media stronghold of newspapers and magazines, and a film production company. This young man understood how imagery and misinformation was used to control the destinies of the people and he wanted to change that dynamic.

The One Nation project was a unification effort to create a coalition of hip-hop artists that shared in his vision under a banner of solidarity. It was to be a collaboration of East Coast and West Coast artists in a sincere effort on his part to neutralize the bad blood that permeated the industry—hostilities that he knew he played a part in proliferating. We were also in discussions with the comedian Paul Mooney, who Tupac adored. This would have been a great project as Tupac was a consummate comedian.

The spirit of service to the people was pumped into his veins as a fetus, as Afeni defended their lives during the NY Panther 21 trial. His dedication and love for the people was sealed passionately in his heart. He was a risk taker, made plenty of mistakes, but never backed down from his truths.

Tupac designed the artwork for the business cards as well as his gold chain and other jewelry.

The design was an angel with a machine gun with a clip made up of black and white ivory keys. It was a metaphor signaling an intent to replace the rat-a-tat staccato of guns with transformative lyrics and spellbinding melodies. It was a noble plan, one necessitating almost magical influence. Tupac had to enchant and lure the people under a spell in order to carry out his will but this is what he did best. Everything he did was multi-layered with hidden meanings. His message of self-empowerment still resonates with remnants of his spoken words, his whispers, his vibrations, his chants that filled the souls of so many—an entire generation still reeling from the unfathomable loss.

Tupac the poet used his rage to ignite the passion in the people. The music industry was a stepping stone. He had the vision to see and the courage to create. We were building a media empire—magazine, film, music, communications.

In 1996, Tupac completed two albums, *All Eyez On Me* and *Makaveli the Don Killuminati*, and filmed two movies, *Gridlock'd* and *Gang Related*. He was finally on his way to building a solid foundation. His work ethic was deliriously exhausting yet profoundly rewarding as he forced everyone around him to dig way down deep inside and find their own glow. Anyone who came in contact with Tupac Amaru came away infinitely more luminous, forever glistening in their own potential. He had a twinkling in his eyes from birth that spoke volumes, like a little firefly buzzing around the room igniting fires in everyone's heart.

I remember coming to the Death Row studios during sessions. He would be so proud to let me hear the new music. Yaki and Tupac were always asking me to play some of my old R&B tunes so they could "hook a beat." They found some real winners—Steve Aronson, Mandrill, Jimi Hendrix. One time when I was driving Tupac home from Can-Am studio, I had the jazz station on. He and Yaki were always changing my station, but this time the old song, "Get Your Kicks from Route 66" by Nat King Cole was playing. Tupac loved the lyrics where Nat calls out different cities and turned it up. He was working on the *All Eyez on Me* album and became inspired to write "California Love" "…from Oakland to Sac Town The Bay Area and back down…Cali is where they put they mack down…gimme love!"

In the studio, Tupac had control. But on the financial side of things with Death Row, it was a whole other story. It was an absolute conflict of interest for him to have Death Row attorney David Kenner representing both him and Death Row Records. Every opportunity I got, I pointed out this conflict of interest but to no avail. Every time we asked for an audit of Tupac's accounts through his lawyer Tree, we were stonewalled. Tree and I both knew there was a lot amiss in Tupac's record label accounting. It was a great concern in my discussions with Charles Ogletree over the next few months. In addition, Tupac had tremendous legal bills from various attorneys handling his numerous lawsuits. Attorneys would contact me because they were not getting paid because Death Row handled all of Tupac's expenses. But from Death Row, there was no accounting, no statements or invoices, just a long list of people representing Tupac not getting paid. There was a lot of money going out, everything being recouped but no accountability as to how the money was being spent. It was a serious issue and I brought it to his attention every moment I could, to the disdain of many.

It wasn't until sometime in August 1996 that Tupac gave me permission to fire David Kenner and interview other attorneys to represent him. It was with much elation I sent the fax to David Kenner signed by Tupac, "Your services are no longer required," and to please forward all legal papers to Tupac's office. I had a few celebratory drinks that night. I was so happy. I proceeded to interview several attorneys with a focus on black female attorneys who had solid experience.

Even while he was alive, for the most part the media has waged a campaign of disinformation and petulant fabrication to intentionally discredit the vibrant cultural movement Tupac exalted. They and all who do their bidding are collaborators in a master plan to obscure the work of one of the most revered icons of the century, while audaciously capitalizing on Who Shot Ya scandals. It is his life that should be celebrated, his spirit and his soul so pure with raw intellect, intensity and courage. Tupac Amaru sprung from the loins of revolutionary ideologists and was raised in a village of exceptional humans. His lifelong aspiration was not to just remain No. 1 on the Billboard Charts or to become the next James Dean. What Tupac wanted was every child to have healthcare, to have both parents in the home, to have food to eat, to live in decent homes, to share in the American wealth, to stop killing each other, and stop being killed by police. How was all of this to be attained? By Any Means Necessary.

His legacy should have endured. In the words of the great historian John Henrik Clarke, "You bury the man and continue the plan." Despite the lectures, the hours upon hours he spent explicating the plans to the "heirs", this dream lost its visionary on September 13, 1996, and was permanently extinguished on November 10, 1996, with the death of Yafeu.

Those who claim their names yet fail to pass on the historic truths have abdicated their responsibilities to which they were entrusted.

(left) Yaki holding his cash outside of the Euphanasia office.

(right) Letter to the 2Pac Family Fan Club.

March 1, 1996

Dear Family Member:

Over the past few months we have been busily reading your letters with hopes of renewing our relationship with you. This task is very timely as we read each and every letter you send.

The Fan Club has recently undergone changes in management and staff and has been restructured to meet the needs and growing numbers of 2PACs many loyal fans. Formerly the 2PAC Fan Club, you are now a part of our family - **The 2PAC FAMILY** and we extend, from our family to yours, an invitation to be the first to get the real DL on 2PACs music, upcoming movies, tour dates etc., etc. We thank you for your letters of love and support through the hard times in 95' and for making **ME AGAINST THE WORLD** a double platinum success. From your letters we see that 2PAC has had a great impact on your lives and continues to give hope and courage to you through his music. We too are celebrating 2PACS accomplishments as an artist and human being in overcoming great odds and we extend a cordial invitation to you, his beloved fans, to come celebrate with us!

2Pac has broken records (selling over 500,000 units the first week, 2nd only to the Beatles 30 year record!) with the release of his new album <u>ALL EYEZ ON ME</u> - the first double CD rap album in history!. Released on bail October 12 pending appeal of a legal lynching 2PAC wrote lyrics and laid tracks for the new album (released February 13) to the amazement of engineers and fellow artists!

A catalogue of general merchandise will be available on April 1. The 2PAC FAMILY basic membership is being offered at a discount along with the following merchandise:

- quarterly newsletter featuring news and updates on 2PAC.
- Autographed picture
- id card (please send passport photo picture when you join)
- T-shirt (Extended Membership only)

Phillip Cox
President

(cut along this line)

Please send $12.00 (Basic Membership); $17.00 (Extended Membership); $22.00 (Outside the U.S.)
DO NOT SEND CASH - check or money order for your Annual Membership Fee payable to:

2PAC Family Fan Club
P.O. Box 480830
Los Angeles, California 90048

Name_____ Address_____
City_____ State_____ Zip Code_____
Country_____ Phone_____
Please check membership: Basic ($12) ___ Extended ($17) ___ International ($22) ___ Age ___ Sex ___
E-Mail Address_____ Suggestions_____

(top) Tupac's crown ring, designed by Tupac himself. The inside is inscribed with his and Kidada's names.

(left) Tupac during a trip twith Kidada, wearing the Euphanasia medallion he designed.

(top left) Spitting rhymes at Thug Mansion, Calabasas.
(top right) Water gun fight at Tupac's home in Malibu.
(bottom) Yaki and Yaasmyn's doggie Louie, Montclair, NJ.

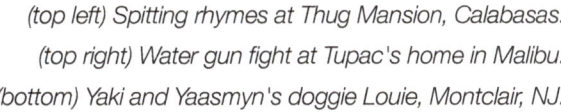

VEGAS - *The Vigil*

As he was valiant, I honor him.
But, as he was ambitious, I slew him.
~ Brutus, The Tragedy of Julius Caesar

I got the call from Tracy Robinson sometime on the evening of September 7, 1996. Tupac had been shot. I remember my first thoughts. It was déjà vu like 1994 when Tupac shot during the trial. I must call Afeni. Heart wrenching to have to break the news to her, less than a year after the first time he was shot. Like that first time I had to make the call to her, the message was the same: Pac has been shot and I have no information.

After that call to Afeni, I stopped at Pac's house, opened his safe, filled a briefcase with cash, and drove straight to Vegas.

When I got to the hospital, Yaki was asleep on the hospital floor. I remember waking him up and hugging him a long time. He was in the car behind Tupac. I did not learn until years later that he gave a statement to Vegas police, without my knowledge, against my wishes, giving a description of the shooter. He was the only one to defy Suge's orders. Yaki had just witnessed his brother getting shot and defiantly described what he witnessed.

I am haunted by the thought that by talking to the police in open defiance of Suge's order may have cost him his life two months later on November 10, 1996.

The next seven days at the hospital were filled with turmoil. Afeni was distraught, but she wanted to take control of her son's affairs. Rightfully so. It was 1969 all over again, Afeni was traumatized and vulnerable, playing right into the hands of the opportunists—media photo ops with the usual charlatans, flocking to Vegas for the cameras. It was a gathering of Crows, using the situation for their own ill gain.

But throughout this ordeal, the Vegas police treated us like criminals, never once giving the impression they were conducting an investigation into the shooting. We were getting death threats daily, the callers threatening to "come and finish the job." I was getting phone calls from everywhere, some with information about conversations overheard, suspects, family, friends—potentially important information. There was nobody in the police department to pass on information to. Nobody to trust. It was chaos. We had no friends there. Of all the places to be—Las Vegas. We did not know who to trust so we had to protect Tupac ourselves.

I went into military mode. There was no way I was going to rely on Death Row security. Where were they when Tupac was being shot?? I contacted Nation of Islam for security and several other security teams and sent them plane tickets. But when they arrived, Afeni promptly objected to their presence and sent them packing, which left us alone and under attack.

We decided to protect Pac as best we could. We rented a huge truck to park outside his first floor, ground level room with windows and took turns securing his life. The press constantly attempted to sneak into his room to take pictures of our dying son. The hospital administration was having a field day constantly primping for the cameras. The Las Vegas Metro Police constantly patrolled and harassed us. They made it very clear they were not present to protect us. They were intimidating and threatening.

**Grab my gats
Locate my comrades
Let's get my enemies
not knowin' I'm comin' back
Let's get my money out the safe
It's time to turn the streets
into a war zone
Soon as I get home**
~ Tupac's chorus from "Soon as I get home"

Yaki was detained and handcuffed outside University Medical Center for allegedly shoving Metro Police gang officers in what was called a "misunderstanding." Photo from Las Vegas Sun.

Son Rize, Volume 1

To die, to sleep, perchance to dream.
~ Hamlet

Son Rize Volume 1 was created in 2005 with me as the executive producer. Michael "D Rizz" Ryan created a masterpiece beyond my greatest expectations. When I met Rizz, he was dating my granddaughter's mother. He was the proverbial OG deejay, with crates on top of crates of vinyl albums: Sarah Vaughan, Miles Davis, Led Zeppelin, Jimi Hendrix…my kind of guy. He was not only a dedicated hip-hop connoisseur but understood the politics imperative to memorialize Yafeu. I gave him the speeches of Malcolm, Kwame Ture, Sekou, Sweet Honey in the Rock–exemplifying the feeling I wanted to capture to honor all our ancestors. Rizz did his magic. Among my favorite tracks are the first and last tracks. The Intro was genius. When he wasn't working on the CD, Rizz handled domestic duties raising the children. He captured my heart with *Son Rize* but when I learned he could braid hair, too, that solidified my respect for this man.

It was as much a tribute to the life of my son as it was a tribute to the men and women whose sacrifices gave us strength and courage. After Yafeu's death, I was in a vortex of grief, a bottomless pit of pain that left me numb to the world. This was quickly replaced by anger at what seemed to be a concerted effort to discredit Yaki's recording contributions in order to minimize royalties. I knew Yafeu was entitled to royalties from his work with Pac but never anticipated I would have to sue my comrade, my sister Afeni, after burying our sons.

Amaru Records, represented by Dina LaPolt, deprived royalties and credit to artists who performed with Tupac by demanding we either waive rights to artist royalties or be taken off the songs. Their position

Donny Rizzo braiding Valencia's hair.

was that Yaki was not entitled to royalties because he was just a "side-man" and that "rappers had no expectation of being paid royalties." I had to retain an attorney and sue Amaru Records, Interscope, Death Row, and a few others in 1997 to reclaim my son's rightful entitlements. Then and continuing to this day, I continue to resist outside claims of ownership for my intellectual property. When you demand ownership of your masters, of your images, and of your legacy, you become a thorn in their side. I made it real clear I was to be the only curator of the estate of Yafeu Fula. I am proud to be referred to as "the difficult one." Nothing more than a feeding frenzy.

It was business as usual in the music industry: screw the artist and sit back and see if they catch it. To be told over and over by the Amaru attorneys that, "Afeni doesn't pay royalties," was more than I could bear. The betrayal was long and deep. It was especially outrageous to learn through audits during this litigation about the numbers of artists on Tupac songs that were denied their royalties, while members of Amaru staff and family received unearned points.

Afeni sent me a bouquet of flowers when I released the CD. She thanked me for honoring our sons' lives. It was her strange way of acknowledging the transgressions being played out in court by her attorneys, unfortunately now making the decisions for her. Their legacy was now defined by percentages and publishing rights. It was a brand-new kind of betrayal, one that surfaces only when the backs of former warriors are broken. I remain resolute.

The passion of the young fans all over the world whose messages of respect and honor for Yaki was an impetus to do this mixtape. It was done to honor him, but to also honor his and Tupac's brotherhood and bond of love. It was to honor the courage of every man, woman, and child on the globe who struggle every day to survive in a cruel world.

For all the youth who reached out to me over the years to thank me for the songs that gave them strength through difficult times—these tracks are for you!!

The opening track on *Son Rize* is a throwback to the music of the 70s from "Black Seeds Keep on Growing" by The Main Ingredient. This first song "Spirit of an Outlaw" is the backbone of it all, for it introduces important events of struggle and resistance that defined our lives at the time. It sets the tone and puts in historical context why Tupac and Yaki connected to the souls of a generation.

This album was created in the midst of many tears and deep anguish. I wanted the world to have something to remember them by, a tribute to their brotherhood, a tribute to the flames they ignited in all of our hearts. It was an attempt to give historical truths about the predecessors who influenced their lives and upon whose truths they relied upon when in the studio penning their lyrics. In order to truly honor their lives then choose courage over comfort and what is right over what is easy. In death as in life, my intentions will always be to honor their lives. Towards that end and throughout their lives…I mask no truths.

TO ALL THE UNREPENTANT TRAITORS WHO BETRAYED: YAFEU WILL LIVE IN THE HEARTS OF THE PEOPLE FOR ETERNITY. HE WAS A WARRIOR AND AS ALL WARRIORS MUST FACE DEFEAT SO HE HAS AND STILL STANDS TALL.

The last track on the album is "Letters to My Unborn" and is a dedication by Tupac to the offspring he wanted so badly but predicted would never see. Had he lived, Yaki's children would have been the apple of his eye. We dedicated this track to Tupac by recording Yaki's daughters, Valencia and Nyasia. They were both seven years old in 2004 when Donny Rizzo recorded them. Donny's verse so powerful, a kickback of ingenious lyrical flow that incorporated their little voices full of enthusiasm and longing.

We even managed to record Yaki bellowing out his infamous wail --- *Yeeeowww, Yeeeowwww!*

Donny Rizzo:
If you're missing your dad, just take a look up to the stars
I'm up above and I'm seeing everything that you are
Don't cry we never die
keep moving for the revolution...

Valencia & Nyasia:
Kadafi lives on
We miss you Uncle Pac
We miss you Daddy Yak
We love you forever.....

Donny Rizzo in the studio with Valencia and Nyasia.

Son Rize Intro

Sweet Honey in the Rock singing the ol' Negro spiritual
    Ain't no one know at Sunrise, how this day is going to end
    Can't no one know at Sunset, if the next day will be here
    Let me sing it now

Radio Commentator
    A pre-dawn raid this morning apprehended members of the New York Panther 21
    Suspects are being tried with conspiring to blow up the Botanical Gardens

Sekou Odinga
    I totally disagree with the expulsion of the New York 21
    I see no reason for the expulsion
    They should be reinstated
    And whatever reactionary forces were the cause
    They should be done away with by any means necessary

Radio Commentator
    All 21 Panthers have been acquitted of all charges

Malcolm X
    No Negro leaders have fought for civil rights
    They have begged the white man for civil rights
    They have begged the white man for freedom
    And any time you beg another man to set you free you will never be free

Radio Commentator
    Militant terrorist Joanne Chesimard….
    Former Black Panther Sekou Odinga

Kwame Ture (Stokely Carmichael)
    If we were listening we would know where we have to go today
    Guerrilla Warfare is where we have to go today

Radio Commentator
    Brinks robbery of 1.6 million dollars outside a Rockland County bank
    Four suspects linked to a terrorist organization have been ….

Jamil Al-Amin (Rap Brown)
    Black people are seriously talking about revolution, not reform. There is no substitute

News Commentator
    Black Panther Sekou Odinga was captured yesterday after a high speed chase through
    Queens left one person dead….

News Commentator
    19-year-old Yafeu Fula, who was a member of the Outlawz Immortalz was found
    Fatally shot yesterday in a housing project in Orange, NJ….

Malcolm X
    We will never forget. You don't shoot one of us and then grin in our faces…
    You don't shoot one of us and then shake our hands and think we forget it…
    No. We never forget, we'll never forget…..someone has to pay….
    Somewhere, somehow, someone has to pay."

Kadafi
    My alias is Kadafi…..
    Speak Drums! Tell the Real Story!!!

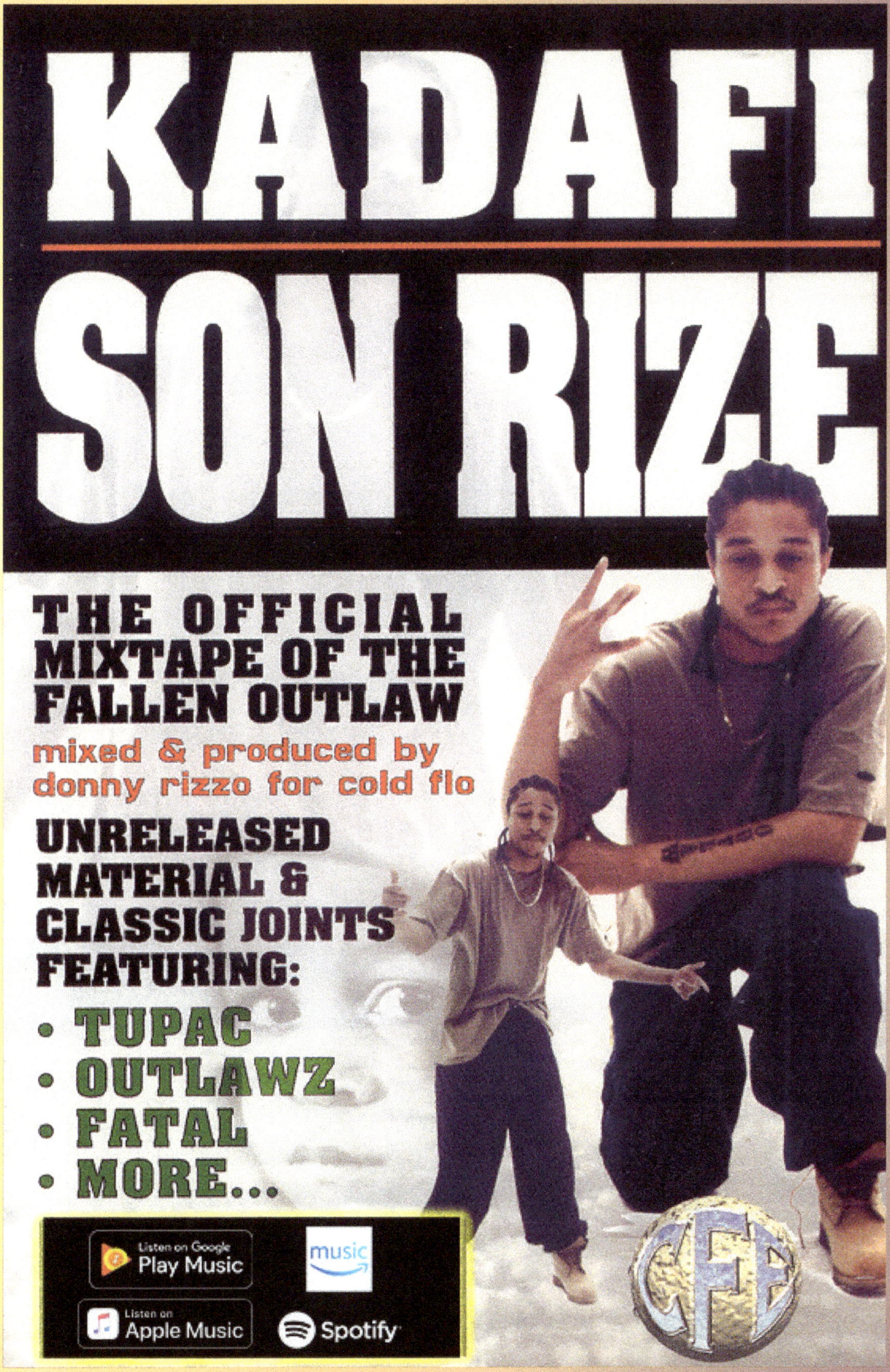
KADAFI
SON RIZE
THE OFFICIAL MIXTAPE OF THE FALLEN OUTLAW
mixed & produced by donny rizzo for cold flo
UNRELEASED MATERIAL & CLASSIC JOINTS FEATURING:
• TUPAC
• OUTLAWZ
• FATAL
• MORE...
Listen on Google Play Music
music
Listen on Apple Music
Spotify
CFE

146

Legacy & Lessons

*"Each generation must, out of relative obscurity,
discover its mission, fulfill it, or betray it"*
~ *Frantz Fanon*

There is so much to learn from this loss. The buoyancy of Tupac and Yaki's lives has been omitted over the years – their vivacity, joyfulness, and devotion to each other. What we can do is learn the lessons from their deaths – their mistakes, their betrayals, and the salacious climate of crime that has become so embedded in hip-hop culture today. So much so that countless young men find it impossible to separate themselves from the hypnotic world of crime, drugs, and debauchery that is annihilating an entire generation. There are Codes of Conduct that have been ignored and what's left is a culture of celebrity worship that adorns itself in self-aggrandizement, misogyny, corruption, and self-destruction.

The radical and revolutionary nature of hip-hop in its beginnings was too enticing for young people to resist. Like countless others, Tupac and Yaki fell victim to this intoxicating and expanding deadly culture. Tupac was intent on using the platform to mobilize the youth to become self-sufficient and participants in elevating their lives and communities. Tupac's fervent desire to give new meaning to Thug Life clearly reveals his transformation and awareness of the fatalistic lifestyle looming so prominently. In the final years of his young life, he embarked on a mission to reinterpret the meaning of the popular term, cleverly redefining it as

THE HATE U GAVE LITTLE INFANTS FUCKS EVERYONE.

In their heart and souls, they knew they must transcend the messages of self-destruction that overshadowed their lives. They reached back to the teachings of their village in order to evolve and carried on the tradition. The tragedy is that neither of them had enough time in their short lives to complete that evolution.

They were both at the precipice of enormous success and made miscalculations in their circle of associations. Mike Tyson, among many, admonished Tupac on many occasions about his associations with some of the worst and most unsavory people.

Tupac and Yaki were betrayed by more than the murderous acts of their assassins' guns. They were betrayed by a system of colonizers whose centuries of conquests and genocide on the people of the planet has taught generations to be bullies and predators. A cycle of home grown American Quid Pro Quo – you hate me, I hate you, I hate me...... THUG LIFE!

They were betrayed by the gallant indiscretions of devoted fathers whose blunders at freedom left them unprotected and exposed.

They were betrayed by a system whose very foundation was built on ancestral blood and whose centuries of systematic colonization decimated nations into submission. That system echoes the message to our youth that bullying, preying on the weak, the different, the smaller, the darker, the joyous achieves power and control.

Both Yaki and Tupac were betrayed by the people they trusted. It is not by coincidence that Yaki's murderer waited until Tupac was dead before he carried out his dastardly deed. Yaki no longer had his brother Tupac to watch over him. According to witness statements, he threatened to kill Yaki one week before shooting him on November 10, 1996, two months after Tupac's death. This 16-year-old predator was the cousin of someone I had protected and introduced to Tupac. The "betrayal oozes out of him at every pore."

The ensuing cover-up of Yaki's murderer with claims it was an accident was refuted by witness statements, medical records, and police reports. It was Blood In My Eye!! As a result, the predator/bully was soon released back to the streets to murder yet another young man quite recently. The deadly cycle of predatory behavior flourishes in the absence of honor, integrity and courage.

How then do we turn these tragedies into triumphs?

The amazing life and legacy of these two young fallen Outlaws should be a valuable lesson to other young men struggling to grow from hood to Manhood. Standing up for truth and integrity in our homes and communities is the first order of business in order to honor their lives and restore dignity to their memories. It is not enough to just bob your heads to the beat. Understand what they lived for, what they died for, and emulate that which you extract as positive in your own lives, in your deeds, in your lyrics, in your hearts.

Yaki and Tupac fulfilled their mission. It is for this generation to now find theirs.

Luxury life results living bad
Tricks of the trade,
Shit that shoulda been taught by Dad
But learned through the crew
Lessons between me and you
And once we lock this shit down
It ain't a thing they could do
Meanwhile I stay waitin' by the phone
Hopin' I get the call
Tellin' a nigga that u home...

~ Yaki's verse from "Soon As I Get Home"

photo by Chi Modu

Black Butterfly

Young, Black, and wild
Lethal soldier with a smile.

A Black spirit too big for his body
A spirit dying to break out to be free.

You are free now Black Spirit, a Black Butterfly
I picture you rolling
I picture you flying, and I smile for you.

Like you smiled for us, young, Black, and wild
You made us all smile.

You live in our hearts; you will never cease to be
Black Butterfly, young, Black, and free.

They thought that you were gone but
they never knew why a spirit strong as yours
can never really die,
that was only the birth of the Black Butterfly.

Young, Black, and wild, a beautiful man-child
who made the world smile and laugh
and cry and think and read, and I ain't mad at you.

You were always growing, evolving, becoming
You were Little Malcolm or Malcolm Little becoming Malcolm X
Black Jesus becoming one with God.

Young, Black, and wild
You made the whole world smile.
You got around
You made old folks listen and young folks dance
And only God can judge you.

When you sang Dear Mama
You eased the pain of millions
Unlocked the hearts of many, like poets always do,
You said what we felt but couldn't say and
We appreciate it.

You are so many things to us,
Poet, Prophet, Thug, Prince, Player
Warrior, Statesman, Artist, Leader, Servant,
Friend, Outlaw, Brother, a Black Butterfly.
Young, Black, and Free
You live inside our hearts, you will never cease to be,
Fly high, Black Butterfly.

I picture you rolling
I picture you flying
and I smile for you.

© Hafiz Farid, 1997

With Gratitude

First and foremost, my grandmother Delia Harrison Martin and my mother Vivian Martin Smith for their wisdom and love.

My granddaughters Nyasia Chanel Key and Valencia Shanel Robinson and their moms, Jameelah Key and Tracie Robinson.

Hafiz Farid for your loyalty, integrity, and wisdom.

Chi Modu ~ deep love and respect.

The Jones Clan:
    Quincy Jones ~ for making that call.
    Kidada Jones ~ sweet, sensitive, and lovable OG eternal.
    Peggy Lipton Jones ~ my special friend – rest angel 'til we meet again.
    Rashida Jones ~ Circle of Women.
    QD3 ~ for all the good memories.

Adrian Vargas - RIP	Ronald Sittler, Esq.
Billy Garland	Sardar Khan
Carol Crooks	Sekou Odinga
Cheryl Davila	Sekyiwa Shakur
Jessica Moncrief	Sharonda Irving
Josh McGowan	Simone McGowan
Lena McGowan	Skye Irving
Lily J. Noonan	Solomon Thomas
Michael Ryan aka D. Rizz	Steven Lowe, Esq.
Nicole Magana	Storm – the Real Outlaw
Ronald "Riskie Forever" Brent	Tony Davila

Last but most certainly not least, all the fans and friends of Yaki and Tupac who continue to keep their legacy moving forward. You are appreciated.

SPIRITOFANOUTLAW.COM
instagram: yasmataz15

OTHER CREDITS

Except as noted below or within the book, all photographs, illustrations, and graphics are from the personal archives of Yaasmyn D. Fula and may not be reproduced without express written permission from Yaasmyn D. Fula.

Courtoom sketches of Sekou and Tupac; courtesy of Marilyn Church and Prints & Photographs Division, Library of Congress.

Exterior view of Lincoln Hospital. Schomburg Center for Research in Black Culture, Photographs and Prints Division; NYPL Digital Collections.

Graphic elements for birthday backgrounds; courtesy of MorganBW; deviantart.com/morganbw.

Map of part of the city of East Orange. Irma and Paul Milstein Division of United States History, Local History and Genealogy, The New York Public Library. (1904) Double Page Plate No. 8; New York Public Library Digital Collections.

Mockup of Makaveli album cover concept; courtesy of Riskie Forever.

Photo of Assata Shakur; courtesy of Angela Davis; democracynow.org/2016/3/28/hands_off_assata_shakur_angela_davis.

Photo of John Carlos at 1968 Olympics by Angelo Cozzi; Mondadori Publishers.

Photo of Tupac and Kidada and photo of Tupac on page 137; courtesy of Kidada Jones.

Photo of Yaki and Tupac on back cover and pages 149-150; courtesy of Chi Modu.

"Playland," Rye Beach: Westchester County Park System, Westchester County, New York, 1927; NYPL Digital Collections.

About the Author

photo by Jessica Moncrief

Yaasmyn Fula was born in New York City, coming of age in the 60s during the Viet Nam war protests, the civil rights movement, days of rage, and the FBI's war against the Black Panther Party. It was during these turbulent years she began her lifelong journey of advocacy for a more just and humane world. Born into an activist family, her grandmother, Delia Harrison Martin, was a well known civil rights pioneer with the NAACP and Urban League. Her mother, Vivian Martin Smith, was a respected registered nurse, health advocate, graduate of Lincoln School for Nurses, and later served as a consultant for the Albert Einstein College of Medicine.

Starting college at Northern Michigan University in 1967, Yaasmyn eventually transferred to Long Island University – Brooklyn campus in 1970, graduating with a bachelors in Sociology. Her desire to be involved in the dynamic social movements exploding across America led her straight to 100 Centre Street: the courtroom of Judge Murtagh, presiding over the New York Panther 21 trial. Yaasmyn actively participated in the demonstrations held outside the infamous Women's House of Detention demanding bail for Afeni Shakur. Out on bail and seeking refuge from the chaos of the trial and divisive Black Panther Party East coast/West coast feud, Afeni stayed with Yaasmyn and friends in New Jersey.

After the New York Panther 21 trial victory, Yaasmyn and Afeni were hired by attorney Richard Fischbein as paralegals at Bronx Legal Services in 1973. It was here they carried on their work organizing against pernicious slumlords of the South Bronx, filing lawsuits on behalf of incarcerated prisoners, and defending the rights of people to live in peace.

The spirit of resistance and struggle was passed onto their sons, Tupac Amaru Shakur and Yafeu "Yaki Kadafi" Fula who were always in tow, tagging along, participating in meetings, demonstrations, classes. Tupac and Yafeu grew up nurtured and emboldened having witnessed firsthand from birth that the template for building a better world comes through empowerment of the people.

At Tupac's behest, Yaasmyn came to California in 1995 to run his music recording company, Euphanasia, with plans of expanding into a full-fledged media/newspaper/entertainment conglomerate. The death of Tupac on September 13, 1996, and then the death of Yafeu on November 10, 1996, destroyed those plans and stripped her spirit to its core.

The call from Quincy Jones in May 1997 to come work for him began the journey of mending the broken wings, giving her heart a chance to resume its former glory and love of life.

Yesterday she survived the FBI's COINTELPRO war on its citizens. She survived incarceration for refusing to testify before a federal grand jury against family and colleagues in Brinks bank robbery in 1981. She survived the murders of her beloved sons Tupac and Yafeu.

Today she carries on a tradition of truth to empower, with the release of her book *Spirit of an Outlaw: The Untold Story of Tupac Amaru Shakur and Yaki "Kadafi" Fula*. Yaasmyn also has several film projects in development and is working on her next book–a memoir.

To live in the hearts of the people is to live immortal.
Long live the Spirit of An Outlaw.

www.ingramcontent.com/pod-product-compliance
Lightning Source LLC
Chambersburg PA
CBHW042033100526
44587CB00029B/4413